# just WORDS Volume 3

## Featuring 42 Canadian Writers

*edited by*
Haley Down, Michelle McLaughlin, and Alanna Rusnak

2019
Alanna Rusnak Publishing

**Just Words, Volume 3**

Copyright © 2019 by Alanna Rusnak Publishing

This book is a collection of the literary works published in the third year of *Blank Spaces*, the Canadian Literary Arts Magazine ISSN 2371-3917. Copyright of each piece herein belongs to the individual author.

All rights reserved. This book or any portion thereof may not be reproduced or used in any manner whatsoever without the express written permission of the publisher and the individual author except for the use of brief quotations in a book review or scholarly journal.

First Printing: 2019
ALANNA RUSNAK PUBLISHING

ISBN: 978-1-7752792-8-0

Alanna Rusnak Publishing
282906 Normanby/Bentinck Townline
Durham, Ontario, Canada, N0G 1R0
www.publishing.alannarusnak.com

Contact the publisher for Library and Archives Canada catalogue information.

Cover art by Kim Duhaime
Cover design by Alanna Rusnak

# CONTENTS

| | |
|---|---|
| Introduction, **Alanna Rusnak** | i |
| Editor's Notes, **Haley Down and Michelle McLaughlin** | ii |
| Canadian Shield, **Erin Alladin** | 1 |
| The Insolvency of Starlight, **Roq Gareau** | 2 |
| Glown, **Craig Clark** | 19 |
| Sunday Morning 9 A.M., **Sheri Singleton** | 21 |
| Down a Thumb, **Zeba Crook** | 22 |
| Monday Afternoon, **Stephanie Tamagi** | 27 |
| Two Divisions, **Emily Fata** | 31 |
| New Departments in Compartmentalization, **Trevor Abes** | 35 |
| Things You Can't Do With a Broken Left Arm, **Cynthia Scott Wandler** | 37 |
| A Dead Black Bear, **Spencer Dawson** | 40 |
| Two Birds People Watching, **Brianne Christensen** | 42 |
| All the Little Things, **Michael Foy** | 44 |
| Taking Flight, **Harvey Mitro** | 53 |
| Cold, **Jordan Ryder** | 57 |
| Lady MacBeth, **Yelibert Cruz** | 60 |
| Romantic Canada, **Mark Halpern** | 63 |
| His Farm, **Sarah Gardiner** | 71 |
| Lupé, a Dentro Del Metro, **Hanorah Hanley** | 74 |
| Somnificance, **Sheri Falconer** | 75 |
| Scarborough, **Kelly-Anne Maddox** | 80 |
| Enlightenment, **Susan Siddeley** | 83 |
| A Luna Moth, **Jennifer Turney** | 84 |
| Grapefruit Break, **Kristin Fast** | 87 |
| I See You, Do You See Me?, **Desiree Kendrick** | 88 |

| | |
|---|---|
| Nightwalking, **Meaghan Hackinen** | 91 |
| The Sandcastle, **Rosalind Goldsmith** | 92 |
| The Bus North, **Erin Alladin** | 95 |
| No Art, **Anna Baines** | 96 |
| No Art Pt 2. Neighbours, **Anna Baines** | 97 |
| Canadian Birthright, **Tamzin Mitchell** | 99 |
| Hometown, **Rachel Freeman** | 101 |
| This Man, **Nicole Schroeder** | 104 |
| Eulogy to that Frozen Banana, **Corals Zheng** | 109 |
| Glass, **Alyssa Thiessen** | 111 |
| Cycle, **Erin Alladin** | 113 |
| Time Infinite Squared, **Jennie Hunter** | 114 |
| Will's Jackpot, **John Alpaugh** | 123 |
| Without Her, **Heather McLeod** | 127 |
| Compassion, **Candace Janelle Ormond** | 130 |
| Surface Tension, **Tracy Evans** | 133 |
| Absent Friends and New Acquaintances, **David Perlmutter** | 135 |
| The Bar on the Hill, **Kim Losier** | 138 |
| Summer, **Hina Rani** | 141 |
| Tokyo Tomato, **Jonathan Mendelsohn** | 144 |
| Defense/Offense, **Hanorah Hanley** | 149 |
| Tweet, **Jessica Kluthe** | 150 |
| Porch Sessions, **Jacalyn den Haan** | 152 |
| The Winter and I, **Erin Alladin** | 156 |
| | |
| Meet the Authors | 159 |

# OUR HOME AND NATIVE LAND
## — *Introduction* —

This summer, I bought a 1981 camper van in an attempt to access the hippie roots I've always had tethering me to a different era. I slapped the back door with an 'I Support Canadian Creatives' *Blank Spaces* bumper sticker and hit the road in search of adventure, travelling a 5000 km loop from home to PEI, down through Nova Scotia and back again. It was a whirlwind trip and it cost a fortune in fuel, but the memories it's left me with are priceless. I gained such an intense appreciation for the Canadian landscape and I understand why it's no wonder it births such brilliant artists and authors. This place is gorgeous! As I walked the Haunted Wood trail in Cavendish, I felt the romantic spirit of Lucy Maud in the trees and knew the narratives to come of that place could never be depleted. In the bustling streets of beautiful Montreal, I felt true poetry. In the colour and buzz of the Halifax harbour I could appreciate the gleaming pallet of inspiration all around me.

We are so blessed to call Canada our home and there's no other place I would want to showcase the work of its beautiful people.

Thank you for being on this journey with me, either as a reader or a contributor. Thank you for the community that has risen up around it, for the continual encouragement, and for proving over and over again that Canada is an artistic force to be reckoned with.

— **Alanna Rusnak**, Publisher, Editor in Chief

# FROM THE EDITORS

As a student at the University of Waterloo I met Pamela Hopwood (assistant editor of *Blank Spaces* magazine and the first two Just Words anthologies), who overheard me raving to another student about my love for fine-tuning written work. Pamela, an effortless connection-maker told me about Alanna and her trail-blazing magazine, and graciously offered to put me in contact with her. Alanna was incredibly generous, offering me the invaluable experience of guest editing the fiction works for their March 2019 edition. I devoured the stories, as I did again when Alanna gave me the opportunity to edit the poetry as well as fiction for the June 2019 edition. Seeing my name printed on the inside cover, and knowing that I was able to contribute a keen eye and to help ensure that those wonderful stories were in pristine shape to hit the printer and get into the hands of the readers was an honour, a great learning challenge, and a kindle to my passion for storytelling. Copy editing this anthology is an opportunity for which I owe many thanks to Alanna, Pamela, and all the writers who have taken the bold leap into materializing these beautiful stories which run wild in their minds, so that us readers may enjoy them immensely.

— **Haley Down**, Assistant Editor

The world seems to spin a little faster now than it did when I was a child. I remember long afternoons of wandering through the fields and forest on our acres of property playing out my imagination with one or two of my dogs and probably a cat along for companionship. As the youngest, with four notably older siblings, I was often alone. But I was never lonely. If my pets or the neighbour kids weren't company enough, I always had my make-believe playmates to fill in the gaps and complete my daydreams. The sweet abandon of being young.

Sometimes now, as the days rush past full of things to be done and places to get to, the world that springs to mind is a hustle. Just as everyone else—whether they are a parent doing their best, a student heavy with assignments, a career focused professional, or any combination of these and more—there is a demand for our time, our focus, and our answers as we navigate both a physical and a digital world. To carve out time to daydream and wander is a luxury that should be indulged in but it often pushed to the bottom of the list.

Sitting quietly and stilling the hustle is how I indulge myself in this phase of my life. As an avid reader, I always have a good book nearby but I don't always have the time to read as much as I'd like and often finishing a book takes longer than it used to. Being part of *Blank Spaces* fills in a bit of that gap for me. I am given the privilege of reading so many varied, poignant stories and poems in small morsels just big enough to fit the time I have for reading. This third anthology is another eclectic collection of written words in just the right sized snippets to while away whatever time you have.

— **Michelle McLaughlin**, Assistant Editor

# CANADIAN SHIELD
## — *Erin Alladin* —
### POETRY

Here where the bones of the earth rise up
In stone above its living skin,
I hear their voices rumbling:
*You once were jointed to us.*

Here where a giant's hand flung lakes
Like jewels across the landscape,
I hear their sparkling laughter:
*Remember you were born from us.*

Here where the woods hold up the sky
And tangle their roots around my heart,
I hear each leaf and needle whisper,
*You still belong to us.*

# THE INSOLVENCY OF STARLIGHT
## — *Roq Gareau* —
### NON-FICTION

I AM STANDING at the water's edge, where two rivers come together. So much of my life can be captured in the confluence of the Maligne and Athabasca Rivers—one half seeking the connection of the other half. According to my parents, I was conceived in this valley. Like salmon, I have made a pilgrimage of return in an attempt to ensure some continuity of life.

Sometimes I'll look at the stars to try and find my significance in the vastness of things. When I give myself to the experience, I'm often delivered a feeling, an image, or a sense of wonder. I get the same effect from staring into fire, eyes, and moving water.

Staring into the blended smear of silty-grey and aquamarine, I see an image of my adolescent-self float by. Rick had taught me at age 19 to whitewater canoe on the Athabasca. It's been 23 years now since I have seen my friend and mentor. That is the way sometimes with men—we tend to reinforce our isolation in isolation. What would Rick have to say to me now as I make the trip from Vancouver Island to the far North for the second time in seven years?

Eyeing another spiral current, I'm transported further back to age

11, terrified and staring into a pool of darkness, desperately wishing for the return of my friends.

* * *

I would have done anything to take or displace my mother's suffering. What was most confusing at age 11 was how easy it was to kill.

I could hear the water running behind the frozen waterfall. I carefully inched towards the edge with a Safeway bag full of puppies. The churning below told me that the unseen pool was not iced over. That's what I was aiming for.

I had to block out my mother's cries and cautions, thrown at me from the safety in which she stood. Part of me wanted to let her projected pain push me off the frosted fringe of the towering canyon. I had to focus on the task at hand if I were to survive this ordeal.

As I pushed my centre of gravity beneath my feet and drew in long breaths, my world grew silent and still except for the concealed waters below and the movement I felt through the handles of the bag.

In that moment, I must have been visited by every boy who had learned to kill. A piercing clarity that exempts all emotion took over. I watched myself hurl the white and red bag into the black mouth of the chasm.

Time had substantially slowed. I waited an eternity to hear the unforgettable slap that continues to hit me as a haunting echo. Half of me died that day.

* * *

I lived in Jasper with my mother the year I was 11. She had just moved back from the East after seven years in a troubled relationship that had taken her away from her prairie home with my father, brother, and me. It was the first time that my brother and I lived in separate homes.

What my mother most needed was a counsellor and, perhaps, a healthy partner. I was neither, but in the seclusion of our lives, I would have to do. As the year advanced, my mom took increasing liberty with sharing details about her past. These unfiltered disclosures were a mixture of pleasant recollections and dark memories. The pleasantries passed easily between us, but the shadowy material began to accumulate inside of me. I was too young to know what to do with stories of betrayal, so I adopted the trauma as my own.

I had a reprieve from the weighted accumulations when we discovered that our dog was pregnant. We had been told she had been spayed, but clearly that was not the case. I remember the day that the seven pups were born. I watched each of the puppies emerge wrapped in a bluish membrane. I'm glad our dog instinctually knew what to do to get each of her young cleaned-up and free from their umbilical cord.

My wolf pack had drastically expanded and so did my joy and wonder. As the pups grew, the cabin started feeling smaller and smaller. We found homes for four of the dogs, but one day my mom announced that we could no longer afford to keep the remaining three. That thought had not occurred to me, and in the shock of the moment, I found myself standing on the impossible edge of a precipice. I did not have the tools or the skills to deal with my mom's urgency, anxiety, or trauma, let alone the darkness of my own.

It was a heavy loss to cut my litter in half. I have ventured back into the recesses of my inner world on many occasions to comfort and assure my child—to help him see that anyone carrying the complexity that I had taken on that winter would have acted in the same way, despite the endless array of other options that have become visible in the clarity of hindsight.

I carried the dead-weight of this wounded boy into my marriage in a red and white Safeway bag, concealed amongst a cache of grocery bags, filled with provisions that made me appear to be a good provider.

\* \* \*

As I returned to my truck and to my present-day 42-year-old-self, I imagined three wet puppies trailing behind, joining me on my northbound journey, to a now familiar workplace, 300 miles southeast of Fairbanks, Alaska. I had spent a summer there, unable to escape myself or my heartbreak, seven years previous, at the age of 35. It was strikingly beautiful, but it was in the middle of nowhere. Off the grid with a generator for power, trucked in water and propane heat, I had my own apartment and was intermittently connected to the outer world by satellite phone and internet.

I remembered that first northbound drive and how I had travelled with a heart full of loneliness and regret. There's sadness in leaving the shores of familiarity. A grief arises when we lose sight of the mainland of certainty.

Five days of driving alone is a long time to sit in your own grief and disappointment. Sorrow introduces you to yourself and prompts recognition that you are not the person you thought you were. I had been in over my head and I was desperately seeking some kind of reset.

I had wished I had the courage to ask my wife to reciprocate financially with our household expenditures—to also get a regular job that could share the load of our mounting debt. We had known that we wanted one of us to be home for the pre-school raising of our children. I had failed to point out that this time had lapsed and that our bank accounts were suffering for it.

I was spent—nearly bankrupt—and my relationship was in crisis. The insolvency had permeated all dimensions of my life. The shame of my financial impotence and my failure as a father and a partner were profound. The fear of the stigma of being publicly seen in my indignity and indebtedness had pushed me to my limits. Something had to change.

* * *

This time, as I drove north, past Jasper Lake, along a braided section of the river, I remembered a dream, set in the same place along the expansive floodplain of the Athabasca valley, that I had had just before leaving the last time.

### Missed Turn

*I am a young man in his late-twenties, standing at the front of a school bus, next to the driver, an elderly gentleman. We are travelling on a quiet highway towards the late day sun. The road runs next to a* large, river-cut floodplain with several channels of swift-moving water. Inside the bus, it is loud with the sounds and smells of many excited children and their lunches. I look back and see filled rows of young people of all ages and gender. The youngest children are at the front of the bus, and the older youth are at the very back.

I am standing with my back to the windshield facing all of the children. We are driving up a steep hill. I hold myself up so that I don't fall towards the back of the bus. As we crest the hill, I look over my shoulder, directly at the sun on the horizon. We miss the sharp turn at the top of the incline and plow through the metal guardrail and fly off the edge of a cliff. In midair, the back of the bus explodes into flames.

Children are screaming and crying in terror as the fire travels through their clothing and hair. I am standing calmly, listening and watching as the screams amplify and the flame moves towards me.

The bus reaches the peak of its arc and then begins its accelerating descent into the floodplain below. It feels like I am falling backwards even though I am still braced upright on the bus. I can see burning seats, bags, and children falling towards me. Just as they are about to hit me, I feel the crush of the nose of the bus striking the surface of the swift-current river. The rest of the bus collapses into me like an accordion, and I am ejected out of the windshield into the dark waters.

From one point-of-view, I experience a complete calm in the whole valley and see the entire scene from an aerial perspective. In another frame, I am in my body, being hammered into the bedrock of the river floor, water moving quickly over and around me. I watch and experience myself breaching the surface of the river and pulling myself onto the dry riverbank. Wearing only a pair of blue jeans, I stand half-naked feeling the cool wind from the northeast on my wet skin and the warmth of the setting sun on my back. Without looking back, I walk into the wind, forging my own path across the floodplain.

*  *  *

At the time I was preparing for the initial journey north, I did not recognize the symbolic resonance of the dream. Only later was I able to draw the parallels to being tossed into a dark pool, and being called to integrate childhood and youth into a single, solitary, and vulnerable man who has the resilience and wherewithal to change direction. It is significant that the driver in the dream embodied a stage of life beyond my own. Driven by maturity, it was an arc of development and an emergent reckoning process that I was after, and it was a lack of maturity (and my blindness to it) that had delivered me to my insolvency.

It was impossible to miss these details seven years later, on the second pass. As I kept driving, I felt a discomfort in my lower back–unease that was now familiar to me. The year after I had returned from the first trip to the North, my wife and I separated. During that year, I started experiencing excruciating and debilitating sciatic nerve pain. The pain ran down my left leg, pushing to the bottom of my left foot. Somewhere in the move and separation, I had herniated a disc in my lower back, which was the cause of my sciatica. Inner disturbance causes outer disturbance. Giving myself to the gravity of things, I was tired and overdrawn on so many accounts.

The most widely-accepted theory on the origin of the word 'bankruptcy' comes from a mixing of the Latin words *bancus*, bench or table, and *ruptus*, broken. When a banker, who originally conducted his public marketplace transactions on a bench, was unable to continue lending and meet obligations, the bench (the backbone of the business deal) was broken in a symbolic show of failure and inability to negotiate.

Pulling myself onto the riverbank of sustainability, out of the current of my relationship, I felt like a broken man. Like in the dream, I had crashed into the river as a half-boy, off of a school bus–schooled in cultural compliance, people-pleasing, and emotional control–hammered by my unlived life. Arriving with the awkward grace of a vulnerable man was a tender accomplishment. The river that I had pulled myself out of was not the same river into which I had naïvely thrown myself. No river, like no human, is ever the same twice. In the careful sequence of time, all of my yesterdays had prepared me for this wounded emergence.

It was very humbling to remember how I had to come to terms with the fact that I had been living beyond my means, financially and emotionally, for too long. As I continued to retrace my tracks, I remembered how that first summer, I had a dream where I woke up trying to reclaim something long lost. This dream deserves a backstory and some history to set the stage.

*  *  *

I turned 35 the month before I first travelled north. Exactly 17 years before that, I had left high school early to start a job in Jasper to work in a remote campground. I had found a way to write my senior year exams from afar and felt as though I had stepped, at least with one foot, into the adult world. I felt like I was at the top of my game.

It was a late afternoon in July when I first met Maria at Kerkeslin campground. She was sitting alone at a picnic table next to a small tent. As I approached the site, the sweet smell of lodgepole pine filled the air. The late-afternoon sun was at my back, but it was Maria's smile that warmed me. Her striking blue eyes, blonde hair and fiery smile were a sight to behold. I wasn't much of a flirt, so I was very practical in the exchange. Maria told me how she and her friend, Jane, who was snoozing in the tent, had hitch-hiked from Nova Scotia. They were heading to Vancouver to go sailing with Jane's uncle—a trip that they had vowed to do together when they completed high school.

What struck me the most about Maria was her fierce, unapologetic presence, her undeniable beauty, and her smile—a smile that etched itself permanently on the stone walls of my heart. As I travelled south to Honeymoon Lake Campground, I could not shake the image of this young goddess smiling at me. I retraced every moment of our encounter: the approach, the smile, locking eyes, words exchanged, and the momentary touch of her hand when she passed me a scrunched up bill for the camp fees. Did she notice the pause when I returned the change?

I couldn't seem to shake the image of Maria smiling back at me. I was quite distracted as I made the first round of collections at the next campground. I knew that there wouldn't be anyone at Buck Lake so I hiked the few minutes from the highway to sit on my favourite boulder next to the lake while I ate the dinner I had packed. As I sat on my solitary stone, I kept looping on the playback of my earlier meeting. The only thing that interrupted the skipping record was the bold agreement with myself that I would talk to Maria if I saw her again.

I finished my meal, took one last look at the moose eating in the shallows on the other side of the lake, and walked back to the truck. The part of me that embraces failure was relieved when I couldn't see Maria on the first pass of her campsite. When I circled back towards the access road to the highway, I could see Maria's face beaming back at me by the light of a campfire.

Maria was sitting on the ground next to a small fire in a metal ring. She waved to me. Keeping my promise was easy. I crouched equidistant to her and the fire and could feel the heat of both the flames and her smile. She asked me how my night was. I told her about the moose and my dinner in that peaceful spot. She smiled and told me about back home, how her brother was a nature nut and had rescued a raccoon and an owl. She found it difficult growing-up with her parents, and she shared that she had lived in Holland with her grandmother for a year.

I told her about Jasper and how special it was. I'm guessing I was already trying to convince her to stay. Conversation with Maria was easy and we talked about real stuff. Night had fallen by the time I left. On the drive back, I savoured the courageous moment where I had passed Maria a small piece of paper with my name on it, a description of how to find my cabin, and the phone number at the campground kiosk where I worked. I had watched her fold up the paper and put it in her pocket with a smile while I described my cabin to her and told her that she and Jane could stay for a bit. They could also have warm showers and do laundry. Behind all of those practical comforts, what I really wanted was to stretch that campfire moment into eternity.

I was late returning to the main campground and Rick, the other attendant on shift, was starting to get worried about me. At the age of 23, Rick was the next youngest employee and, of all the staff, I got to know him the best that summer. He and I shared a passion for music and we got along well. Our shifts overlapped a lot, and we got to take the work truck into town after work on Wednesdays to gas up and get supplies.

Rick asked me why I had returned so late. If it were anyone else, I would have bit my tongue, but with Rick, I spilled the beans. He looked at me and said, "Well shit, when do I get to meet this Mona Lisa?" I didn't know how to answer that, but I just smiled as I cashed out.

The next day, Rick and I worked a cleaning shift together. As we scrubbed washrooms and outhouses in the morning, he recounted the story of his first sweetheart and confided in me that he was hopelessly in love with his best friend's girlfriend. By the early afternoon, while scraping the ashes out of fire pits with metal shovels, I told Rick that although I had, at one time or another, fallen in love with half the girls in my high school, I never had the guts to follow through with my feelings. The potential always remained in the realm of fantasy. Rick saw the significance of my talking to Maria and mirrored that back to me. He told me that she'd be stupid not to take me up on my offer.

By end-of-shift, my statistical calculation of whether or not Maria and Jane would show up was starting to push the odds against my favour. The part of me that thought of myself as unlovable just shrugged and said, 'I told you so.' I sat with Rick at the picnic table in the outdoor space between our cabins. We laughed together as we rested from our workday. "Just you wait," he said. "Just you wait."

As I washed the soot off my face in the shower, I imagined that Maria and Jane had already made their way north to the junction with the Yellowhead Highway. I paused for a bit, watching the water pour off my hair. I stayed that way in the shower until I was done crying.

I put on a new set of clothes, dried off my hair, and made my way to the open front door of my cabin. I could hear several voices laughing, and as I looked through the doorway, I could see Rick followed by Maria and Jane, both with big backpacks on. Maria's smile brought a smile to my face, and when I looked at Rick as he walked up my steps, he pulled his fist in front of him and drew his elbow down in a silent, 'YES! I told you so.'

The closest I ever got to Maria was the morning she left, when I wrapped both my arms around her, stretching my fingers beyond the black tank top covering her bare shoulders that were still warm from a shower, and kissing her once on the forehead. I felt her give herself to the caress. I wish I could have done the same.

Jane and Maria arrived on a Tuesday and stayed until Friday morning. I worked during the days, but once I clocked out, the three of us were thick as thieves until bedtime. Rick and I drove to town at the end of our shift on Wednesday. I dropped Rick off at the underpass on the edge of town so he could walk the tracks to his friend's place. I saw Rick in a different light then, knowing that he was walking into a bittersweet triangle in which he and his best friend loved the same woman.

When I met up with Jane and Maria, I was taken by their excitement to see me. As we walked through town that evening, I had never seen so many heads turn. I got a real sense of what it was like to be in the company of a star.

I worked the next day and made a simple dinner of roasted chicken and potato salad for me and my new friends. Later that evening, I mustered the courage to ask Maria if she would go for a walk with me. She accepted. That was the only solo time we spent together, other than the evening we met.

We walked down the road to the oldest part of the campground, next to the river. I wanted to show Maria my favourite sitting spot. We dangled our legs off the 15-foot cliff above an eddy whirlpool on the Athabasca River. There was just enough light to see the bleached skeleton of the old moose carcass beneath the swirling water. It had to be pointed out; otherwise, you'd never see it. You had to focus on the top edge of the antlers and soften your gaze beneath the backspin of the river for the bones to reveal themselves. I had first seen the bones on a bright sunny day when I fell into a trance-like meditation watching the confluence of counter-currents while contemplating the flow of life. I hadn't exposed the aquatic grave to anyone else. It was special to me. I asked Maria if she would stay in Jasper for the rest of the summer. I knew the answer already, and I respected her pact with Jane and the unchangeable timeline for their once-in-a-lifetime sailing trip on the Pacific Ocean with Jane's uncle. I wasn't prepared for Maria's counter-proposal: that I join them on the fiery adventure. The invitation stirred my imagination beyond imagination. However tempting it was, a line was drawn within me, and I knew at that moment, if I crossed the great divide in pursuit of Maria that it would inevitably end in heartbreak and disappointment. She had an ability to fly close to the flame, meeting fire with fire, with dexterity and courage that I couldn't match. To follow Maria would be to fly too close to the sun. I was not prepared to sacrifice the wax wings I had laboured to create.

I had all night to say silent goodbyes, so in the morning, I left much earlier than I needed to. I wanted a bit of time to compose myself in the campground kiosk before starting my day. The tenderness of the kiss I gave Maria's forehead was the best of me I had to offer in that departing moment. Her smile was gone and so was mine. On our next cleaning shift, Rick told me that I had made the right choice, but I knew that he would have said this regardless of which path I had chosen.

\* \* \*

I knew I would return from that first trip from the North with a plan to file for bankruptcy or with enough tucked away to strike some settlement with my creditors. To maximize my returns, I was cautious with money that summer. For my last set of days off, I decided to prudently stay put and squeeze some ink into my journal to make some sense of my life and my impending return.

I had just completed a set of shifts and I was exhausted. I had spent my evenings that week mapping out the names and last known locations of people who had had a significant impact on my life. Part of my process that summer was to complete a sort of life review, recognizing relationships of consequence along the way. For those that I had lost touch with entirely, I accessed what little internet bandwidth was available to me to do Google searches of names on my coffee breaks, sometimes narrowing searches with locations or occupations. Most people left a trail of breadcrumbs; several had no digital presence whatsoever.

When I got to Maria's name, I couldn't find anything at all. As I worked, I made up the story that she had married, changed her name, and moved to Australia; although, Maria was not the marrying or settling type, and was more likely to live full-time with a dog than another person. She was part gypsy, part daredevil, and all free spirit. On my next break, I did a Google image search of her name, knowing that I could spot her stunning smile and fiery eyes in a sea of images. Sure enough, about fifty thumbnails deep, there she was.

I clicked the image, and it brought me to a public Facebook page with the title: *In Loving Memory*. My mind raced to take in the new information. Was it true? Wait, was it her? Yes. Unmistakably, yes. There was a single picture of Maria playfully smiling back at the camera at age

14 or 15, in a yellow T-shirt and blue jeans. I read the text below the image: *In memory of an amazing person lost to all of us at the young age of 25.*

On the one hand, I was utterly shocked–how could I have been carrying a story of Maria alive and well when she had died ten years earlier? What happened? What was her life like in the remaining seven years after we met? On the other hand, I was not at all surprised. We have many pop culture examples, particularly in music, where a person's genius pours out in a celestial explosion that extinguishes their luminous output prematurely. Whichever perspective I held, it left me feeling unsettled. Ten thousand slight interceptions of fate might have prevented me from crossing paths with Maria again, but this one sealed it.

On the eve of my final days off, I skipped a late supper and went straight to bed. That night, I had the following dream.

### *Follow Me to the Ocean*

*I wake up in my Yukon bedroom and it is light out, as it always seems to be. I have a feeling that someone is watching me. I look off to my right, and Maria is standing next to my bed, piercing me with her bright blue eyes. "Wake-up sleepy head," she says before I can even say a word. Maria reaches out with her left arm, and our fingertips link in the sunlight. "C'mon," she says with a warming smile as she pulls herself out of the room and lets my hand drop. I spring out of bed to not lose sight of her. Maria is halfway out the front door when she pauses for a moment and says, "Follow me to the Ocean!" She continues walking down the front steps, out of sight, leaving the door wide open.*

\* \* \*

I woke up with a flinch because I was in the same place I started in the dream. This time, I didn't see Maria, but I got up just as quickly because it felt like she was still close.

That hidden sweetness of Maria's smile that once opened a space between us in the sun-extracted pine scent of Kerkeslin campground was retrieved from an obliterated past and warmed my Northland apartment.

Chance meetings are always one part inner essence of people, one part outer essence of place and two parts mysterious trouble seeking resolution. The blend of all the parts colours the relationship into the future, possibly forever.

Things become clear when you begin doing them. I realized when I was packing the car that I was going on a road trip. I felt like the world, or at least my world, was now tilting towards the Pacific Ocean, and like water, I was going to discover the path of least resistance. I unconsciously left the passenger seat empty. The intentional space only made sense once I started driving. That's where Maria was sitting.

That summer, like this unexpected road trip, was about reconciling debt, which even required repaying an invisible loan that I didn't even know was there. With Maria beside me, I felt closer to a sense of adventure, confidence, courage, and purpose than I had in a long time. She left the door wide open and made it easy for me to embark on the quest that I wasn't able to accept 17 years earlier.

For the soul, it's never too late. The soul is more interested in the ripeness of time than the straightness of time. At one point, I put my open hand on the centre console and caressed Maria's hand in mine. In that waking moment, the untouchableness that was enforced with finality in the former days dissolved.

I told Maria all the things I wish I could have told her in Jasper before she left with Jane. Things like how beautiful I thought she was, especially when she smiled, and how her passion for life and intimate friendship with Jane inspired me. I also told her how much of a big deal it was for me to talk to her and to invite her to stay, and how grateful I was for her and Jane's visit. I told her harder things as well. I spoke of how I could tell, particularly when she retreated into a deep inner space and lost the sparkle in her eye, that her early life carried complexity and trauma, which was amplified by her parents' disapproval of her exuberance. I told her how I was envious of her worldliness and easy way with people. I confessed that I was ultimately afraid to chase someone whose spirit was so big and unattached. Sometimes the hardest thing to do is to articulate that which we know to be true and assume others know as well.

I found a beautiful walk-in tent site just below the foot of Exit

Glacier, near the port town of Seward, Alaska. I set up my two-person tent and put my backpacking Thermarest inside with my sleeping bag and pillow on top. I crawled into the tent, said goodnight to Maria, and went to sleep in a satisfying exhaustion.

I woke up early the next morning and didn't recall any dreams; I just knew that I needed to spend the day on the water. I made my way to the waterfront and bought a ticket for a day cruise. The water surrounding the Kenai Peninsula was calm and the sky was perfectly clear. I still felt Maria strongly on my side. Within me, I felt the excitement of a child. We saw pods of humpback whales and colonies of sea lion, flocks of puffin, porpoises and a black bear. The highlight for me was seeing and hearing glaciers calving into the ocean. The rumble sounded like slow-moving thunder and it was visually stunning. Glaciers really are slow-moving rivers.

The boat returned to port in the late evening. When I arrived at the campground, I noticed a group of campers using the cook shelter, but in my fatigue and introversion, I walked directly to my campsite. I scanned the site and entered the familiar walls of my tent. I drifted off thinking about the day at the front of my mind and, at the back of my mind, wondering who I would be had I followed Maria all those years ago. I quite liked my life and the person I was becoming. I knew that any sharp deviation from my path would have led me to a different life, so I didn't dwell too long in those thoughts before sleep took over.

The next morning, I woke up knowing that I would be hiking up Exit Glacier to the Harding Icefield. I grabbed some warm clothes, put on my stiff hiking boots, and packed some extra food for the day. The trail started out flat but the pavement ended quickly, and the steep ascent began. The last three miles were in snow. I didn't know if I would make it. I could feel my feet blistering after the first two miles. It felt important to make it to the plateau of the Icefields, beyond all visible footprints.

I found a scenic place to stop for lunch on the expansive icefield that fed 35 glaciers. I had to strip out of my sweaty clothes, into some dry pants and a jacket. Clouds were rolling in and the wind was picking up. In the naked white truth of that arctic wilderness, I began to cry. I had a slight shiver and my feet were throbbing, but there was much more to this overwhelming sorrow. I cried for my forgotten sense of adventure and courage. I cried for my displaced passion for life. I cried for all the layers of loss that were haunting me. Mostly, I cried for the loss of Maria.

I felt bare-boned and swirling in my grief as I flashed back to the moment all those years earlier on the edge of the Athabasca River, pointing out the underwater moose skeleton to Maria and putting my arm around her. Well-expressed tears have a way of swimming upstream in the river of time to dissolve past hurts and reveal misplaced brilliance. I didn't hold back; there was no one there from the land of the living to hear the cries of my upriver pilgrimage.

When the tears were through, all that was left was an apology to Maria for converting her into a deity and projecting my passion, starlight, and gold onto her. That's a lot to carry for a flesh-and-blood woman, especially one who has her own fiery excess of spirit. I made the request that we return what we had each carried for one another. At that moment, the clouds drew in and the wind whirled. Overtaken by the melancholy of the dark sky, even the solitary companionship of my shadow had left. I felt a strong gust of wind at my back, pushing me down the mountain. I returned alone.

Suffused with the spark of my displaced longings, the trip down over the snow-covered parts was a lot faster and easier. The rain started about half-way back. When the snowpack turned to mud, the burning pain of my raw heels set in and intensified with every step. The final stretch felt like the longest mile of my life. A descending somberness has a way of scrambling a sense of distance.

After removing my boots and blood-stained socks, I put on some flip flops that I had stashed in the trunk of the car. As a symbolic meal that night, I bought some roasted chicken and potato salad from the Safeway deli. I ate it with my hands while parked at a viewpoint looking up at Exit Glacier. The glacier had a mystical white glow to it, as though it were a bridge between worlds.

I wasn't excited about making my way to the wet tent, but I knew that it would be dry on the inside. As I lay alone under my shelter with my spine touching the ground's reliable caress, I felt like a piece of a puzzle returned to its rightful place. I could feel my backbone had a newfound strength and integrity. It was hard to get comfortable with my thrashed-up feet, but I gave myself to the earth's tender embrace and fell asleep quickly in the welcomed darkness.

That night, Maria returned to me in a dream. She came into the tent and thanked me for the trip, kissed me on the forehead, and left.

I woke up to the sound of a torrential downpour. The edges of the tent were already wet and, afraid that the nearby river might become so swollen it would take me out to sea, it was my time to go. I unpegged the tent, collapsed the poles, and folded the whole wet mess into the backseat of the car. Anything that I wanted to keep dry I put on the passenger seat. It was no longer occupied.

The arc of my return began with my drive back alone from the Kenai Fjords. My time in the North had led me to my frontiers of discovery to find anchorage within myself. Within three months after returning home, changes started happening. I narrowly escaped bankruptcy and started therapy with a psychotherapist. I was in the rapids of my life, and wobbly as it was, it was much better than being a petrified glacier, frozen in a dull and a rigid sense of duty, breaking instead of flowing. During that time, I had the following dream:

### Out of the Woodwork

*I am watching myself walk through a forest of very tall trees. After walking for some time, I come upon a meadow that houses a small wooden cabin with a plume of smoke coming from the chimney. I approach the cabin as though I am meant to be there, and as though I am arriving right on time. I step onto the deck and in through the door. The space is warm and inviting with simple, rustic, but well-used furniture. Stepping into this wood-finished environment is like stepping into the heartwood of an old growth tree.*

*I notice a large pot filled with liquid darkness on the stove top. Beyond that is a well-lit room with a large wooden table. My grandmother stands next to the table and motions me to come closer and sit next to her. As I walk over to the table, I am very much aware that my grandmother is the oldest living relative in my direct bloodline. We sit down and face one another, and she takes my hand in hers. As we look into each other's eyes, no words are exchanged, but out of the woodwork, people pour into the room. Impossible wooden staircases emerge from all of the walls, floor and ceiling, and people start walking in from all directions, as though emerging from an M.C. Escher drawing.*

*I am aware that all of these people are simultaneously aspects of me and also my ancestors. Grandmother and I listen as they each speak in turn and they collectively offer a complete, multi-perspective review of my life. When the review is done, Grandmother's warm hands let go of mine. Grandmother stands up and goes to stir the pot of darkness, and this time, in it, I see stars.*

\* \* \*

Properly rendered with the capable manipulation of an elder, stars belong in perfect darkness, where their brilliance can be soaked up and genius tempered. As I prepare to return home from a second summer of brightness in the far north, this time as a divorced man with adult children, I'm struggling to find where I'm meant to direct my brilliance. Every now and then, I catch a glimpse of three healthy feral dogs on the arctic tundra. They are neither wolf nor dog, but I get the impression that they won't be returning home with me. They are home.

I often don't feel as bright as I'd like to be, even though I shone my starlight to make space in the dark places where I've buried secrets in shallow graves. I always thought that by the confluence of midlife, I would have more answers than questions. It turns out I was wrong, but I also never thought my need to understand everything would also wither with time. There is no safe way to live life. That is why I have my eye on a star that I will passionately chase into the second half of life. This time, I will gaze into her fire and be moved by her current.

# GLOWN
## — *Craig Clark* —
### FICTION

SOMETHING LINGERED in the thing she said. I could never let her last words go. I was constantly dissecting each syllable and searching for promising inflections. Noise echoed through the moonlight. It vibrated the white walls of my hotel room. I was sitting alone with my back against the headboard. The wood rattled every time I moved. The curtains flowed into the room as the rhythm bounced past the thin white cotton.

Stay beautiful.

Four syllables. She hit the word hard, emphasizing the *st* sound. Her vernacular stumbled together almost like she was forcing it out. There's no point looking at her face. Sound came again. It was a more persistent mix of moans. What is this? Loaded jubilation? The carpet squished under my feet. I breathed in the contaminated evening breeze. Persistent moaning. City lights filled my view. Traffic is faint mood music.

St - ay beau - ti - ful

She wasn't even looking at me. Her eyes were rolling around the room, down the hall, and into the street. Bouncing as they leaped off the curb. Weaving in and out of cars. Spinning through people's legs. At the end of the street they turned right and disappeared into dusk. Smack, smack, smack. Is it moaning or groaning? I'm sure there's a difference. A groan is more associated with pain. A moan is more sexual. I'm not sure it matters.

    Stay beaudiful

A *t* is a *d*. Maybe it's more meaningful to pro - nounc - i - ate words. To really capture every sound of each letter. Screw diphthongs and digraphs. I want to hear each letter. That's more respectful. A *t* as a *d* means speech is an afterthought. When does obsession move on? It's like the radio, nobody knows when or how, but eventually it will be new. Beaudiful is you. Then you walked away and rolled into dusk.

    Stay beautiful

Where were you going? It obviously didn't involve me. Somewhere in the dusk you ran away. Left me with words that have less meaning with every time I think about them. My lips and tongue don't move the way they used to. And I apologize.

    St

        a

            y

        be

            a

                utiful

Confusion is something we talk about. To be confused is to be mindlessly intoxicated with afterthought. It always feels like winter and all concrete looks the same. I can never tell the difference between curbs, sidewalks, and streets. Salt has bleached them all to a similar shade of drab.

# SUNDAY MORNING 9 A.M.
## *— Sheri Singleton —*
### POETRY

Sunday morning, 9 A.M. breakfast noises from the kitchen
And a televangelist from the living room
Preaching hellfire and damnation for the wicked
While my father whistles over pancakes,
The closest thing to enter my mouth to the Host;
The pancake syrup, my sacrament.

It's a good day. The whistling makes me brave.
Brave enough to pad from my room to turn the knob on the TV,
Volume down but not off, no need to push the limits.
And there's bacon too. He's on his meds?
No, he's just up.
Wide eyes shining. I love this version of my father
The version that makes breakfast on a Sunday
But I know that close behind comes the father that
Once held a bottle of pills to his lips and stared straight into the hellfire
The man who can't be saved by a thousand pancakes, a million
    strips of bacon,
Or one daughter's love.

# DOWN A THUMB
## — *Zeba Crook* —
### NON-FICTION

HE HADN'T exactly shouted this time, but still I jumped, and regretted it immediately. He liked to see me startled. It would toughen me up, he promised. Really, it was for my own good.

"I've told you. A hundred times. Both hands." There was a curse word or two thrown in there somewhere, wedged out between clenched teeth. I was grateful. When he cursed, he wasn't really mad yet. It was when he stopped that I worried.

I hated being told how to do my chores, to use both hands on the axe, but I said nothing. He approached and I took half a step back, my stomach tensing. He took the axe from me with one hand and wrapped his other around my arm until his stubby, calloused fingers met.

"See?" he said as I winced. "You're not man enough."

Then as if to prove the obvious, he pushed me backwards, then to the side, and then pulled me toward him, like I was a rag doll, his toy, seeing if he could goad me into pushing him back. I never pushed back.

The fir round I had been trying to split fell off the block when I took my hand off it. He had to move his left foot deftly to avoid it, and I pursed my lips and swallowed hard to stave off the grin that threatened to warm my cheeks.

"Do it like this." He picked up the round from the woodshed floor and placed it on the block. He rotated it several times, muttering at it to stand on its own and cursing some more, but the top of the chopping block was so mangled and uneven that the piece of wood could not stand unassisted. Bending over, he picked up a few chips from the floor and wedged them between the round and the block, looking over at me to ensure I had taken note. I was looking out of the woodshed, thinking of how Charles Atlas promised from the back of Archie comics to turn any skinny scarecrow into a barrel of muscle. How he handled that guy at the beach once he was stronger.

"Hey," he growled, snapping his fingers like he was a hypnotist pulling me back into reality. "I'm not telling you this because I like the sound of my own voice."

In a tone that aspired to be gentle, and with the round finally stable, he instructed me. "Both hands, aim for the centre, it doesn't even take that much force." He had a point; the rings of the piece of wood became smaller as they reached for the centre, giving the round the appearance of a target. If you hit the bull's-eye, the round splits every time. But it was never easy for me to hit it.

He raised the axe above his head with both hands. It seemed he did nothing more than let it fall through the air, merely guiding it to the centre of the round. The piece of wood fell contentedly in two perfect halves, one on each side of the chopping block. I wanted to pick them up and hold them together, just to see how perfectly they might fit. I could see the top of one of the pieces, and swore there wasn't even an axe mark on it. Perhaps the round had taken it upon itself to split in the instant before meeting the force of the axe, sensing the futility of holding itself together. What's the point of integrity?

My mind wandered to a punchline without a joke: Hey, that axe is coming, let's split.

He held out his hands to me. I didn't get it. I stared blankly, looking around for a joke to go with my punchline. Then I got it: I was meant to see ten whole fingers. He wanted me to think he always chopped wood the safe way, with two hands on the axe. But I'd seen him use the axe one-handed. And I noticed all the knife scars on his hands from the other work he did.

"Your turn." He lay the axe on the woodshed floor.

I went to the cord of wood he and I had stacked together but had not bothered to organize, to look for another fir round.

"Birch."

With heat starting to flush around my temples, I put the fir back and dug around for a piece of birch.

I placed it on the block and quickly bent down to find a chip, but the round stayed in place. Smiling triumphantly, I reached for the axe. It was my turn to raise the axe above my head. I tried to look as capable as he had, wishing I were stronger, always wishing I had been stronger. Then, with all the force I could muster, I hit the round. In my head, the axe whistled as it moved through the air, a sure sign of its precision.

Three inches off centre.

In the corner of my eye, I saw the right side of his face, from lip to eye, give that familiar twitch of shame. It said, *not good enough*.

I knew it would be trouble getting the axe out of that tough piece of birch. I hated birch. I knocked the whole thing to the ground, and with one foot on the round tried to wrestle the axe out. It was no use, and I was sick of the fight.

With the round firmly secured to the axe, I swung both above my head, bending my knees slightly to get underneath it, and in that sweet spot when something held above your head seems to float on its own, I flipped them both over with an ease I was proud of, and smacked the back of the axe against the top of the block. The force split the round in two uneven pieces, victory enough for me.

I was surprised to see a look of warmth on my step-father's face. He was looking down at the block.

"That's why it's in such shitty shape," he said with a heavy heart. "Beats the hell out of it when you do that." He ran his fingers over the beaten wood, like he felt remorse for how I had abused it. He walked away without a word, leaving me to finish my chores. I was ninety-seven pounds, and it was getting dark.

\* \* \*

I always warmed up for races carrying my track spikes in my hands. They were so light I barely noticed them, and it saved me from going back to my bag and facing my teammates before a race. I didn't like the last minute wishes of luck, the admonitions to "Go get 'em."

My legs wobbled a little as the eight curving lanes of red track came into view through the high green fencing. I had finished my warm-up through unfamiliar forest trails, keeping the stadium sounds close. I sat down heavily on the grass outside to stretch. The brick-heavy feeling in my legs would go away, I trusted, when the gun went. It was a constant and necessary trust, the kind you cling to, for without that trust you don't start races.

I entered the stadium and went immediately down to the track. I slipped my running shoes off my feet, and then my socks, and put on my track spikes. I loved those spikes, red and yellow, one colour bleeding into the other. I slipped my T-shirt off to reveal my racing singlet, blue with stark square letters of my school in yellow across my distance-runner's chest. It had been slightly damp after my warm-up, but it was dry now.

I went to one of the heavy steeplechase barriers. It wasn't right to call them hurdles; it took two men to move them, and they didn't fall over like hurdles if you hit them. I touched it with my hands. It was painted black and white, but there were little holes pierced through the paint from runners' spikes, making the small fibres of its wooden heart visible. Poor wood, I thought. If the runners were stronger, they would hurdle over you, but instead they step on you. I always made peace with the barriers before a race. I had never run into one, never smashed a knee, but I had heard the anguished cries of those who had from behind me, usually toward the end of a race. The wood wins every fight.

Then I saw him at the fence. Black beard messy, hair unkempt, my step-father looked homeless as always. But he had come after all, and that was something. I went over to the fence. I was on the downhill side, but still I was taller than him. I was surprised to be so tall and to feel strong. There had been the occasional phone-call, but it had been a while since we stood face-to-face, I realized.

Years later I would see a photo he took just after this moment, of me walking away, back turned to him, head down in concentration, arms loose and ready to run.

"Coming in?" I asked. "You still have time."

He shook his head.

It wasn't the ticket price, I knew.

"I'm ready," I said. I wasn't nervous anymore. And I was stronger now.

The announcer's voice, calling the high school boys to the track, boomed suddenly through the speakers directly above our heads. I jumped a bit. It made him smile, and me too.

"I'm ready," I repeated.

I wondered if he might try to say something. I paused for a second to give him the chance. But he didn't. He just nodded, like he knew he didn't have the wisdom to say just the right thing, and that I didn't want to hear it from him anyway. I wasn't sure why exactly, but I would have shaken his hand if there hadn't been a fence between us.

I went to the start line and paced, my legs feeling light and the other boys starting to gather around. They were all strangers to me, from other schools around the province. Those closest to me shook my hand. We were men now, we thought; this is what men did. I looked down at my own mismatched hands.

Both hands on the axe. His voice is always there in my head, reverberating. It was a mistake I only had to make once, the day the end of my thumb joined the chips and dirt and goat shit and dog hair that carpeted the woodshed floor. Oh, and the blood; I can still see it shooting to match my pulse until I choked it off with my right hand. My stepfather was upstairs carving a design into a ring when I screamed, his knife marking its own thirst for blood on his hand. He entered the kitchen ready to explode, and I braced for the shrapnel, but he saw I had it the worse. Victory enough for me.

Everything in the stadium turned quiet. I stood still and straight, eyes looking out at the track ahead of me. I loved this moment. Soon the starter's commands would come, to place our toes on but not past the start-line, and to wait for the sound of the gun.

I did as I was told.

I waited to run.

But really, I was already free.

# MONDAY AFTERNOON
## — *Stephanie Tamagi* —
### FICTION

IT STARTED started with her purse. All my life it hung by the door on a brass hook, containing no more than a lipstick and her wallet. Over what seemed like weeks, it started to overflow. She'd extract dirty forks, half-eaten fruit, and torn pieces of the newspaper. I would find it in the sink, hung in the pantry, in the den next to the African violet she'd had for a decade, suddenly wilting with brittle leaves. She became suspicious, asked me if I'd taken it.

I began by pulling out old photographs, the dusted albums she used to force on me when I was young. She used to narrate every faded snapshot, laughing at her clothes. I thought it would help keep her here with us, with me. Over time she grew quieter as I flipped the stiff pages. A week before I brought her here, I found them in the trash.

She's coughing hard again today. I know the jutting knuckles of her spine, the hair that grows across her skull like a fine mould along the curve of a trembling eggshell. It used to be long and auburn. She would tug at the ends when she was nervous, curl it on Fridays, and use it to tickle my nose until I giggled.

In the beginning, she often regarded me as a stranger, sometimes animated as I entered, asking questions and offering me tea in her nightgown. Her eyes would dart into the room's corners looking for the kettle, for the wrapped sour cream cake she made every week.

"Forgive me, I seem to be unprepared for company. What did you say your name was?"

"My name's David." Kills me every time. *You named me David so that I could fight giants, you always said so...*

"David, it's so nice to meet you... You'll have to forgive me. He'll be here any minute." Looking past me to the door, expectant.

She spends her days now waiting; paper-skinned hands adrift in her lap. I'm in the same chair with the cracked rose vinyl and uneven legs. I can feel the tick of the watch on my wrist, the marching of the gears, the warm hum of whiskey, flask pressing against my thigh. Two heavy swigs before I walk in every Monday, the rest is for after I leave.

"How are you today?" I've stopped calling her Mama because it can confuse her. My question, though formal, is without names or salutations.

She doesn't answer, doesn't even move. I've learned not to ask too many questions. It could take her all afternoon to reply, or until the next visit, or when I'm not here tomorrow. My words fade to the place where everything goes. There's a place where phone numbers, Levi being in jail, and my face all live now.

"Not sleeping well, but better the last couple of days." It's the nurse who walks with the limp, always smelling of coffee, with bleached hair like straw.

My mother has found a way to protect the man she waits for every day, having let go of everything else. I'm not sure when I realized she wasn't talking about Dad. She never says the man's name and I never ask. The last few visits she doesn't speak, and if she does, it's of him. Last Monday she was placid, speaking in fragments. They call it 'lucid'. It is a word she would have liked, the sound of it.

"He talks in his sleep. He's always asleep before me, and I hear him mumble things, sometimes he says my name."

"That's nice. That's good." *What did he call you? What was his voice like?*

"We're always so hungry." Her mouth curves into a half smile. "He always has cheese and apples, pieces of bread wrapped in his pockets.

Yesterday we rode his brother's motorcycle. Have you ever ridden a motorcycle?"

"No, never." *How did it feel?*

"My father threw me out because of him... said I was cheap, that I didn't belong to the family anymore. Do you have a cigarette?"

"No. No, I don't."

We used to escape to the bench in the courtyard and share them. I'd never seen her smoke, the sharp inhales, and her shoulders relaxing as she blew it out in a straight stream. The last time she forgot where we were. We don't leave this room anymore.

"We broke the washing pitcher... his mother's... porcelain with a blue painting. I have a piece with a cottage roof and the branch of a maple. I know she'll miss it, but I can't bring myself to return it. Isn't that silly?"

She grasps her fingers at her hip, where she used to keep it in the pocket of her apron. I remember her holding it, comforting her palm with its smoothness. She made me run and get it before she went to the hospital to have Levi. I remember her hissing through a contraction, her fists gripping the cheap wood of our kitchen table, Dad fumbling for his keys.

She turns towards the nurse, lifting her arm to get her attention.

"He's like strong drink. A man's heat can be like that. It can make you stumble, like something inside you is trying to catch its breath." The nurse smiles and casts an uncomfortable glance towards me.

"I miss him no matter how long he's gone. It could be minutes, and it's like there's a hole inside of me."

I think of all the minutes in a lifetime.

"We're going to get married. We can't decide whether to go to the city or back east. It doesn't really matter either way."

I don't know if she's ever been east. Until now I thought the furthest she had been was to Dad's family farm outside Melfort. I wonder if east means Winnipeg, or Trois-Rivières, maybe Nova Scotia. I find myself awake at night, realizing just how much is east of where we are. I wonder where he came from, where he went, and why he gets to keep her, even now.

I dread the afternoons when she thinks he won't come; the threat of a misery that could engulf her. Time has moved so quickly it has left pieces of her behind. She asks where he is and I watch the agitation rise in her throat. I want to hold her, press the pieces back together. But she screams if I try to come near her with a panic that makes me sick. I've learned to lie with a fervour and conviction that eclipses everything else.

I've learned to tell her that he is on his way, he will be here. He called and will be late. He has a surprise for her. I tell her that he could never forget her. I tell her it's all going to be fine.

As if I know, as if I'm sure.

If she believes me she will stop crying, her wet green eyes suddenly bright. Of course, he's coming, must have been held up. She'll look out the window again, fold her hands, and wait.

In that moment, she's gone again. In that moment, it's as if she was never there.

# TWO DIVISIONS
## — *Emily Fata* —
### NON-FICTION

SHORTLY BEFORE my twenty-first birthday, I became hell bent on destroying myself. It wasn't because I was turning another year older. My boyfriend had dumped me well before spring came earlier that year, carelessly tossing me to the side like our past seven months together had been relatively unimportant, if not utterly meaningless. He was all of my firsts, beginning with my first kiss and diving head first into everything else. He had made me feel like I was radiating with life, swiftly unfurling for the world around me with new emotional and sexual awakening. *And now what?* I am a broken castaway. I am a thought that has slipped easily and suddenly from the mind.

I knew I could not change the fact that I was broken, but I could ensure I was not silent, just as I knew that although I was a forgotten deliberation, I could be an entirely new notion formed of an unsullied desire for a novel me; a phoenix blinking through the ashes of her well-worn past as she rises up to... To what? Ah, to becoming hell bent on destroying herself, of course. Every element must become a contrast of all that she once was. This is the most beautiful kind of metamorphosis.

The level-headed and observant girl I was in those days before I met him, with time and practice, became a woman who was both reckless and brash in her daily interactions with her environment. This new woman stayed out late to walk along the streets alone, eyes alternating between downcast to searching for a challenge. She courted danger simply for the sake of it, because it gave her something exciting to do. Yes indeed, this was her convoluted perception of excitement. Exhilaration often came in the form of squinted eyes at strangers passing by, exasperated sighs over professors' voices in the middle of otherwise silent class lectures, and insatiable road rage. That is, when her mind wasn't consumed with thoughts of *What if I drove into oncoming traffic at this very moment?* or *What if I veered into that light post?* or *What would happen if I pulled over to the side of the highway and ran into the road as cars approached?*

    The girl who only drank socially and was always smiling morphed into a woman holding a bottle of wine in one hand and a glass in the other, knocking back drink after drink before succumbing to fatigue, finally falling asleep, the light from the open fridge door casting one side of her face into shadow. I thrived off of the notion that I could go home to an empty house and drink my wine straight from the bottle if I so desired. I often did. There were nights too, when I slipped into a gin-induced lull, the spiked tonic water entering my system like an intravenous, the only sound my muffled sobs as my mouth parted against the rim of my glass. Those were messy days... Those were the nights when I questioned my transformation and doubted that I was doing the right thing in trying to change myself so completely instead of placidly accepting my fate as it came. The more I regretted my conversion into the New Me, the more I pushed back against Myself. I was Jekyll and Hyde, an innocent host encumbered by an unshakeable malevolence that crept from me with such ease. I was a living and breathing opposition to myself in the pursuit of becoming Me.

    I was the girl who quietly simmered in frustration from her ex-boyfriend's flippant attitude toward recreational marijuana use, becoming the woman grinning devilishly as she sprinkled ecstasy into her Coca-Cola. My just frustration over how I quietly accepted his inability to attend a single party without getting high faded as I gulped the soda down, being cleansed with twisted self-satisfaction. I could not feel the carbonation stinging my nose and burning at my eyes, or hear my friend telling me to slow down. The only sound I could fully register was the victorious *Yes* hissing from my parted lips as I crushed the red plastic cup against the table we had been sitting at. *I've one-upped him*, I told myself giddily. *I did it.* To me, I had taught him a huge lesson, as well as showed myself how much superior to him I was and always would be. I can do whatever I want, whenever I want to. I am single. I am free. I am free. I am *free*, goddammit.

These self-declared accomplishments tended to reign over my consciousness whenever I felt my composure slip—whenever I remembered that I was the one brushed off like dust to the wind—and tears threatened behind my eyes. Once upon a time, I would go take a shower so that I would never know just how much I had cried, my tears intermingling with the spray over my naked body, shivering despite the water's warmth. I would find myself sitting on the floor of the ceramic tub, wailing into my knees gathered against my body, my hair matted and stringy under the downpour aimed at my back. I knew wholeheartedly that I had to commit to this, or I would begin to retreat and eventually abort my mission.

Now, I dealt with these slip-ups with my newfound vices. Gin washed away my anguish just as easily as showering and if you drank at a quick enough pace, it pacified much sooner. Still though, each time I saw his name come up on social media, I felt my heart flutter with desire, my stomach twist in pain, and nausea rush over me. My body revelled in its hell. It exulted in the bitter agony each image of him bestowed, the way the brain protested the very idea of being severed from something that had once seemed as permanent to me as it had felt secure. I latched onto the life he portrayed over his various profiles as earnestly as I cast aside my own persona. Past Me and Current Me were the perfect example of dichotomy; we were a separation into two divisions, differing widely from and certainly contradicting one another. It was bliss. I shoved my way violently through the cocoon of quiet isolation that I had wrapped myself with in an attempt to heal my wounds, ready to put into action my best recovery strategy. Now, here I am.

This girl that I was had pushed herself into her twisted idea of adulthood until it became thoroughly customary. I strived to forget whom I was when I was with him. Sometimes, I found myself praying that maybe my Harbinger of Firsts would want to take me back—be *my first rekindled relationship*, be the successful consequence of *my first desperate attempt to wrestle with loneliness*—that maybe the New Me would not be so easily let go of. Other times I hoped this innovative construction of myself was everything he hated, the opposite of what he had initially fallen for. I wanted him to hate me as much as I hated him for casting me aside. In the very least, I wanted him to care enough to notice that I was someone completely different. *Just please, please don't see right through me.*

The more that I thought about it, the more I realized that this was not the root cause of my warmly embraced downfall. Neither he, nor love in general, nor a combination of the two was my hamartia. No. *Life* was my hamartia; living was what was obliterating me, the experiences that were thrown my way, that were wiping out my sanity one blow at a time. This was me fighting back. This was my ability to jam my middle finger at Existence. *Try and stop me now.* Each person I pushed away, each drink I chased with yet another, each drug I felt swim though my body, each new boy I let cast his mouth around mine, they all worked toward setting my mind on an expedition bound toward alleviated emotions. Can one not strive to forget? Is that so wrong?

In time, I began to forget the roots of my despair (or interchangeably: anger, resentment, self-pity) and was focused in the most effusive manner on my sole task of gradual self-destruction. I wanted to have the full experience of it. This was the final 'first' he would give me—this salaciously tantalizing desire to shed my own skin—and I was going to welcome every single second if it until it finally consumed me. It could have been a couple of weeks after I had decided upon this journey, even a few months. I would soon be entering the seventh month of my Retreat from Being and, with astringent acceptance, I acknowledged that we had been apart as long as we had once been together. Disintegrated. Fragmented. Divided. Crumbled. Words like sweet, sweet venom coursing through my very veins and trailing their viciously gentle fingers along the vessels of my brain. So many dichotomies, but I was the most impressive one, by far. I was a disjointed whole.

# NEW DIRECTIONS IN COMPARTMENTALIZATION
## — *Trevor Abes* —
### SHORT PROSE

Jake Burckhardt, overnight merchandiser at my hospital gift shop, makes enough money to lose $700 in savings per month. To remedy this, he hosts thrice weekly sessions of what he baptizes SDT (Structural Demystification Therapy), where the goal is to get in the black by getting people to appreciate a job he can't stand.

He thinks about fractals each time he rents the run-down hall and lines its perimeter with shelves, tables, and sundry fixtures, and covers the floor with boxes of multiples of random cheapo items from garage sales and Value Villages.

Around happy hour, the fruits of his targeted ads pile in to relieve stress through the luxury of having things just so, of enjoying complete control over a space for which they can fully realize a vision. There are portable spotlights for Instagram and acrylics of various shapes and sizes to aid a greater pool of showcasing aesthetics. If anyone is having trouble getting started, Jake is available to Socratic method a direction out of you.

People's work reflects what they've been meaning to leave behind. Charlene Hanania, recruiter for a travel agency, tied a clothes rack with shirts on which she hung hangers. Selvon Lentl, pigeon breeder, made pairs of long bookends out of horizontal romance novels and lined them down a bookcase, leaving space down the middle for six copies of *Oedipus Rex* in consecutive stages of a twirl. Maude Behn, freelance echinacea farmer, filled a slatwall fixture on wheels with picture frames she'd emptied and poked holes through to look like eyes. She strung Christmas lights behind the sockets and wrapped the structure in layers of bubblewrap until the glow dulled into a tentative curiosity.

Participants may retain the rights to their sculptures for a small fee or split profits from sales and exhibits with Jake, minus venue rentals. Completed works are open and available to the public for as long as session attendance allows. Franchising opportunities available.

# THINGS YOU CAN'T DO WITH A BROKEN LEFT ARM
## *— Cynthia Scott Wandler —*
### NON-FICTION

1) Scratch yourself anywhere outside the reach of your right arm, such as your right bicep, tricep, or that damnable itchy spot on your right shoulder blade.

2) Time travel back to before you realized you were going to hit the concrete hard, before the snap and the pain, the hollow you felt at your elbow with your other hand. Time travel back to that morning so you could stay home instead of going out, to before you screamed from your side on the gravelly pavement, eyes closed against everything but the sickness in your stomach and arm, helplessly waiting for someone to call 911.

3) Thank the strangers shading you from the white bulb of the sun with umbrellas from their cars, even though when she arrives the EMT snarls, "Move those away so I don't get poked here."

4) Wear the wedding bands the surgeon needed a ring cutter and pliers to pry from your swollen finger once you were finally sedated, before your upper arm bone was forced back into its elbow socket while the woman in the waiting room, hearing your

yells, said to the man sitting across from her, "That poor woman," to which he replied, "That's my wife."

5) Stop crying when the surgeon tells you, the day after the break and dislocation, while you sit in a wheelchair with a pillow supporting your cast, that if you want to be able to use your arm normally for the rest of your life, you need surgery. A metal plate and five screws to hold your elbow together, in fact.

6) Tell people how it really happened. Because unless they know what your daughter has been through, and what you've been through as a family, they will not understand, and will judge you, and her. Even then, they still might.

7) Not fantasize about returning to the children's hospital emergency room you were at five months previously, to find the psychiatrist who saw your daughter then. Where you would carefully lift your broken, bruised, sliced open and stitched up arm, now titanium and bone, before his face and say, "See? I told you someone would get seriously hurt, and that we were here asking for your help before that happened. And all you could say to us, while my child cried, asking what the point of living was if she always felt that way, while she begged us to help her, and you ignored her, was, 'I don't know why you came. I don't know what you think we can do. I don't know why you're here.'"

8) Clip the lengthening, widening spades at the ends of your fingers, formerly known as fingernails.

9) Dress yourself.

10) Work.

11) Watch the entire season of "Breaking Bad" on Netflix without using a chopstick to reach the buttons on your laptop, so as to remain in a comfortable position, where your arm does not conduct an orchestra of wailing nerves each time you move.

12) Stop shaking your head against the disbelief that this is even happening, after all the doors you have knocked on, the professionals you have met with, the programs you have accessed, the help you have sought for your young daughter, the rest of your family, yourself.

13) Spend the night in the same bed as your husband, because

you won't sleep for fear he'll bump your arm during the night, the same reason he won't sleep.

14) Put your bra on. Which is why you will proceed to wear it overnight, every night, when your husband goes back to work, without the satisfying release that comes at the end of the day when you unstrap, so your almost-12-year-old son doesn't have to look at Mom-areolas through your T-shirt or tank top during the day every time he sees you, causing him to avoid you rather than visiting with you during your brief forays to the couch, or when you need him to bring you water to the bedroom.

15) Pull your hair into a ponytail or do anything with it other than let it air-dry into a dull, rumpled curtain.

16) Hold it against your daughter, even though while you're lying on the concrete and she asks you, "Mommy, are you mad at me? Mommy, are you mad at me?" you think you want it to sit with her a little while longer and maybe it's okay you can't answer her.

17) Defend yourself well when she threatens to break your other arm.

18) Overhaul the malfunctioning public health care and school systems, to establish instead: Compassion. Competence. Intercommunication. And Funding that is as far-reaching as the problem itself so that those with a brain illness can be clothed in the layers of assistance they need—like having underwear, socks, pants, a shirt, a jacket, a hat, shoes for warm weather and boots for cold—rather than one ill-fitting, greyish tube sock with a hole at the big toe and the foot seam that rubs, which is the existing system.

19) Massage the parts of your daughter's brain that cause her to rage, coaxing them to rearrange themselves so she experiences

joy sometimes,

and peace,

and regularly more happiness than sadness and shame.

# A DEAD BLACK BEAR
## — *Spencer Dawson* —
### FICTION

IN THE the forest surrounding our town there are terrible things which cannot be explained. They say anyone who steps foot under the trees is vulnerable to them, but it is the loggers who suffer the most. No word but 'soulless' can describe a man who no longer speaks a word, looks you in the eye, or shows emotion of any kind. For this is the suffrage of the victims. They go on living, even return to work, but anything inside of them that could have been called human is gone.

Those with souls left to lose live in fear of the forest one day taking theirs. Only the valuable hardwood that comprises it is able to draw them inside.

In our town there is passed down a way of trapping whatever it is that steals men's souls. It requires a dead black bear, shorn of its fur and painted with pagan writ be hung by its hind legs from a high branch. With some luck, in a night or two when it is lowered down, the dead animal's eyes will be blinking wildly; long believed to be the struggles of an ensnared possession. Tradition tells us to cut out the frantic eyes on the spot.

But that was tradition. The new century has brought with it a new world that has replaced animals with steam, livelihoods with industry, and superstition with capitalism. These days land holders pay thirty dollars for the complete bear, eyes intact and blinking. The crown offers an additional five for proof of that transaction.

In an effort to allay fears within their workforce, the holders hang the bears in the camps and along the river down which the loggers ride the great felled trees. These deeply traditional workers count each bear as one less spirit left in the trees.

Just as the timber trade it seeks to protect has brought real wealth to our isolated town, the bounty system has helped raise my family out of squalor. So as it begins to collapse in grotesque fashion, it is my home the woodsmen amass in front of, it is to me they direct their screams. The bears come alive on their stakes, they say, the soulless are cutting them down. Sure enough, out my window, I see a pair of the hairless beasts chasing down the elder Mrs. Sherborne, the least decayed of which quickly succeeds. In the moonlight I can still read the words I wrote on it.

I grab my rifle and load it before the mob breaks down my door and fills my modest home. They see the rifle and tell me the bears cannot be killed even by gunfire. It's not for them, I mutter, turning the barrel upwards under my chin.

# TWO BIRDS PEOPLE WATCHING
## — *Brianne Christensen* —
### POETRY

Chickadee musters up courage,
comes within five feet of me,
thinks his curiosity makes him brave,
scours the rained-on
ladybug-gumboot-stomped-on earth
for his next meal.
Me? I'm slouched
on the however-old milkcrate in the driest corner
of the U-Pick Check-In-Station where my only job today,
thanks to the summer squall, is to slouch
on the milkcrate,
stare at the rain, the birds, the dirt
and swallow a pound of fresh strawberries
that my discount gets me for 30% off.
I think something vaguely deep
about wanting my next meal to taste kind of like Truth.
I'm not really sure if poets ever get to know what that tastes like
or if we ever get to stop
looking.
I toss a berry out onto the dirt;
does that make me a better person
than Me Ten Seconds Ago? Chickadee
flutters a little ways back, then scurries closer
in that smug bird way that aims to prove something like *I was never
    really scared.*
People do that too, I guess.
My eyes are held open by the two cups
of coffee I sipped slowly around 6:00 a.m.
I'm looking at Chickadee
who's looking at the berry.

I'm looking at the owl-shaped weather vane that glares
at both of us with a rusty
vengeance
like it's our fault that we've got flesh legs, feathered wings, fresh
　　berries
and something more than hollow eyes.
Blink.
Chickadee disappears into overcast skies.

# ALL THE LITTLE THINGS
## — *Michael Foy* —
### FICTION

SEVEN-YEAR-OLD James Seeley climbs onto the kitchen counter, stands and reaches into the cupboard for a stack of bowls. Blond hair, like broken bits of straw, frames his face. Reginald Seeley pours coffee into a mug, leaving room for milk, and slides the carafe back onto the warmer. Scratching the top of his shaved head, he flips off the switch.

Still standing on the counter, holding his cereal bowl to his chest, James shifts his gaze. "Dad, have you seen someone die?"

Reggie stops stirring his coffee, lifts and drops the spoon. *Clink.* "You know I don't like you climbing up there."

Reggie wears a blue Correctional Officer's uniform, his duty belt is fitted with a flashlight, handcuff case, and key clips. He's used to having everything within reach.

"What are you having, son? Shreddies? Mini-Wheats? Or your fave, Cap'n Crunch?"

Usually distraction works, but James is too old now.

"Cap'n Crunch and the big spoon. *Have* you Dad? Have you ever?"

Reggie blinks several times. Correctional Officers are taught to mask emotion. Feel it and let it go. Never wear it on your face. Reggie looks down at his boy's bare feet, at the arches, high like his mother's. He pours

Cap'n Crunch into James's bowl. Two of the little orange squares escape and drop to the floor. James slides from his chair and crawls under the table.

"Careful Dad, you might crunch them with your boot."

"Get up here."

But James keeps talking. "Donnie Corgan said you help them die. Is it true?"

"Donnie Corgan's older than you, isn't he?"

"Grade Four. He showed me on his iPhone. All sorts of pictures of the people at the prison, all dressed in orange. What's a strap-down team and why do you hold their ankles?"

Reggie has to remain silent about his work on the Execution Team—code blue. Reggie thinks that Steve Corgan, Donnie's dad, must have had his head entirely up his ass during that part of the training.

Reggie misses Carol. His wife would have intervened here, saying something like, "Hurry up and finish that cereal, let's get you ready for school," ushering James away from the table while tucking his hair behind his ear. And James would listen. Carol would have been there after school, kissing the top of his head and wanting to talk. She gave James all the little things he needed, but Carol Seeley died four years ago. Reggie remembers how he always sat in the chair next to the hospital bed with his legs crossed at the ankle, while James slept beside her and the tumours spread. Some nights, she read his favourite stories, using all of her wacky voices—slow to build suspense and quick on the action. Everything she loved around her.

There was a futility in the IV drip, the injections, and the monitoring of vitals; in James being told he had to move from the bed, and the sound of the privacy curtain sliding on the rod—opening and closing for the nurses, the bed bath and plastic food trays. Her weight kept dropping, until she was only bony cheeks. After six weeks, Carol's bed was wheeled to the family bereavement room. What if Reggie had opted for Critical Illness Insurance? Could that clinical trial and a new course of treatment have stopped the spread?

"Later, James, later. We'll talk tonight. Get off the floor and finish your cereal. I poured the milk. It'll get soggy."

"Cap'n Crunch never gets soggy."

James slides back into his chair, scoops up a spoonful, crunching and slurping at the biscuits bathed in milk.

"Remember son, no bus home today. We have a meeting with Mrs. Redding. I'll see you out front of the school—got it?"

"Got it."

"Put your lunch in your backpack. That school bus ain't waitin' for no one."

\* \* \*

They stand at the entrance of the Blue Valley Trailer Park waiting for the morning school bus. This is new to Reggie's routine. He hates the wait, the lack of control. They face the rows of empty concrete pads in the lower half of the trailer park, each with a picnic table and a grey post bubbled by a hydrometer. The evenly spaced posts are like an army of robots awaiting command. Most of the summer campers are gone, migrating their RVs to winter storage. The grass gleams in the dew and the day is quiet, except for the sound of tires on gravel when the Park Super drives past on his golf cart, giving the horn a couple taps. *Beep. Beep.*

"Mornin', gents."

"Mornin'."

The school bus rolls up next and the driver yanks the silver handle, springing the door and popping the flashing stop sign into place. Reggie follows his son up the steps. He scans the passengers while the diesel engine chugs in the background, and he sees every face but Donnie's.

"Hey, Mel. Just looking for little Donnie."

"Didn't get on."

"Oh, okay. James won't be on the after-school bus. I'm picking him up."

Reggie's about to get off when two kids in the front row notice his uniform: the duty belt, the badge, the vacant radio hanger, and the wide brim on his grey trooper hat.

"Mister, you got a gun?"

"Hey, you only carry a gun when you're on Tower Duty or escorting prisoners off prison grounds."

"That's sick!"

Reggie steps off; the bus drives away. He takes his Ford F-250 to the staff parking lot at the Washington State Prison, takes his duffle bag from the box and checks his watch: 7:43. He's missed the morning briefing. He flashes his ID and they buzz him in. He grabs the briefing summary from his mail slot, checks out keys, a radio, and rubber gloves. He scans the bullet points:

- Scissors found in cell 404 confiscated and removed.
- Barbed wire near the south fence parking lot, second to last stall—bent, unable to straighten by hand.
- Two Charlie Seven lost one hour of Rec for talking during quiet time.
- Tom Wilkie's Retirement Party. Early release for good behaviour! The Green Lantern Pub this Tues 7 p.m.

Reggie walks into Bravo Pod to relieve Officer Corgan.

"Okay, Seeley, all your equipment's here. You got an upper and a lower coming out today. Head count of 89. Your run-arounds are Thompson out of two and Moralez out of six. And today *is* Wednesday, so you *do* have uniforms."

Steve Corgan hands the clipboard to Reggie, who slams it on the desktop. "What the hell is your problem?"

"What?"

"You gotta rein Donnie in. He's showing James all sorts of shit online. Donnie told him I'm on the strap-down team—on the strap-down team, for Christ sake!"

"Look, Seeley, I got enough problems right now. Raising the kids is Lenora's job."

"Yeah, well, James is non-stop. And how does Donnie know so much anyway?"

"Google Washington State Executions—I dare ya. You can see it all right there on Wikipedia. There have been seventy-eight executions since 1904, last meal, final words—the whole nine. So when Donnie asked me if I killed one of those men, I said, 'Damn right we did, two criminals, and we got eight more to go.'"

"Get rid of the cellphone. He's in Grade Four."

"Lenora wants it to keep track of him. Our kids will find out eventually. Is that what's got you so riled up?"

"Maybe that's it."

"You know what they called it before it was Capital Punishment? Judicial Homicide. Kinda points the finger at someone else. And these drugs are all screwy too, you know it, you remember how Cal was. I say we get back on the grid and just zap 'em."

It was true. After the first injection, Cal Thomas coughed and heaved for close to thirteen minutes, struggling to breathe, his left eye slightly opened and staring out at the world. Corgan pinched his right arm before injecting the pancuronium bromide and Cal's right hand shook as if his bird tattoo wanted to flutter from his wrist. Corgan pinched Cal's wrist before the potassium chloride, and his index finger began to twitch, pointing everywhere in the room.

Reggie says, "There's something wrong with the whole operation when we're the only ones walking in and walking back out again. When I started working here they never asked me how I felt about wheelin' away a body."

"Tell James you have a minor role: two leather straps and a pair of buckles. It amounts to nothin'. We're silent actors."

But Reggie wants to talk about how often he hugged Cal Thomas through the bars. How, over his seventeen years of imprisonment, Cal was a big part of his daily routine. That magnetic chessboard and all those matches, their moves exchanged on a lunch tray napkin. *When I play, I live so many lifetimes.*

On execution day, as Reggie was buckling him in, Cal nodded, eyes closing slowly, as if to say: "It's okay, what you will do to me."

\* \* \*

James is sitting on a blue bench outside the school office, waiting for his father.

"I told you to meet me *outside*," Reggie says approaching from the hall.

"I know, but Mrs. Redding asked me to wait here."

"Hello Mr. Seeley," Mrs. Redding says, coming from the office. "Why don't we go into the conference room across the hall." Mrs. Redding walks back to the staff room. "Mr. LeGarry, let's get started." She turns back to Mr. Seeley. "I invited Mr. LeGarry, our school counsellor."

"Fine with me."

"James," Mrs. Redding says in her soft voice, "we need you to wait out here while we talk to your dad. After that, we can invite you in. Is that okay?"

"Yes."

"Here," Mr. LeGarry says, walking past James and placing a small box on the bench. "I know you love Star Wars Lego, see if you can build this one for me."

James stares at the X-Wing Fighter, rattling the box. "Cool."

Mrs. Redding leads the men into the conference room, leaving James on the blue bench.

In the room the blinds are closed; a long boat-shaped table takes up most of the space. A muffled whistle and shoes squeaking on the gym floor can be heard through a wall.

"Please," Mrs. Redding says, "take a seat. Thanks for coming, Sir. We have some concerns about James and his schoolwork. His journal entries have us worried. As you know, James is still developing his writing skills, but his drawing is quite detailed for a boy his age. Mostly he sketches death and dying."

She opens the journal to a page marked with a pink sticky and spins the book to face the father.

"And this content is certainly not related to anything we cover in our curriculum."

Reggie examines the drawing. Most of the white space is filled. It is the interior of a room, a lemon coloured light fixture hanging from the ceiling. Several men, sketched in brown and black crayon and drawn with heavy eyebrows, big noses, and tiny mouths, stand around a woman lying prone on a table. Each person is holding an object—a piece of something, a part of someone—it's hard for Reggie to tell. The woman on the table has Xs for eyes. Reggie flicks his fingers across the drawing, knocking away bits of pink eraser. "Kil all her!" is scrawled into a dialogue bubble with a black marker.

Reggie removes his hat, turning it upside down on the table. The sweatband is moist and a stain marbles the liner.

"Mr. Seeley, would you like a glass of water?" Mrs. Redding asks.

"I'm fine."

Reggie draws a long breath, exhaling through his nose and crossing his arms.

"Mr. Seeley, we're worried. We know that Mrs. Seeley passed away about—"

Reggie raises his hand. "Mrs. Redding. I'm not sure what to say," he says, tapping the picture with his index finger. "It's not right for my boy to be drawing pictures like this here."

Mr. LeGarry offers, "Well, Mr. Seeley, we think James might be experiencing what they call complicated grief—"

Again, Reggie raises his hand. "Look, Mister, I appreciate your concern but I'm not the one... I mean I'm not. You see, Carol took care of James when it came to his schooling."

The conference room door clicks. A thin white line appears at its edge. Everyone turns and the door swings open, as if pushed by an unseen force. James runs in and dives under the boardroom table like he's jumping from the edge of a swimming pool.

"James," Reggie says. "Come out from under there, son."

"I heard," James sniffles. "It's not fair to look at my stuff."

"I see," says Mr. LeGarry. "Come out bud, so we can sort this out."

Reggie pushes his chair out, peering under the table. His left hand trembles.

"Damn it! James Andrew Seeley, don't make me crawl in there to get you."

James is looking out at all the action around the table, the moving legs and feet, chairs on rollers. They're coming for him. He moves to the centre of the table. It's a chase, and he's got a hiding spot.

Mrs. Redding's voice is softer than the others. "Honey, we were just about to invite you in. Come on out sweetheart, so we can talk."

James rubs his eyes. His breathing picks up and blood moves to the surface of his skin, flushing his face. His dad pushes chairs, circling the table, looking underneath for a way to get at James.

Tears roll from James's eyes, his nose drips, and the more he wipes, the more slime smears across the back of his hand.

Mrs. Redding and Mr. LeGarry hunch over and look at James between chair and table legs, like a viewing gallery, letting Reggie do the work. Reggie moves closer and from his stomach he lunges, but James moves right, so he misses. Reggie tries again, this time he clamps onto his son's right ankle and shuffles backward on all fours, dragging James out.

"Leave me alone! You took Mama like this. Because, because Donnie Corgan showed me. And you're in trouble now!"

Reggie lets go.

James dashes over to Mrs. Redding, who kneels, wrapping him in her arms. The shame of hearing the accusation introduces a silence to the room. Reggie doesn't want to be a part of this. He can get up. He can leave.

"I think it best if we end this," Reggie says.

Mrs. Redding nods, wiping James's nose with a Kleenex. With her hand at his back, she guides him closer to his dad.

Reginald Seeley reaches for his son's hand, and holding it, realizes again how small it is. Reggie puts his trooper hat back on his head. Leaving the boardroom, they enter the hall.

Basketball practice is over and the players are at the far end of the hall taking turns jumping and trying to touch the exit sign with one finger. The hall echoes with, *Sweet! You got this!*

Outside, rain and darkness fall from the clouds broiling across the sky. Reginald and his son walk to the truck. Despite his grip on James's shoulder, Reggie feels it all slipping. His whole life. Fatherhood. Everything. Every damn thing.

The musky smell of cedar drifts in from a clump of trees at the edge of the lot. Reggie opens the passenger door and lifts James into the booster, moves around to the driver's side, opens it, drops his hat on the seat, and gets in. He puts the key in the ignition and turns off the radio. He leans back, pressing his fingers to his eyes and rubbing circles. Reggie's tears soften the edges, making the images swell and recede, like looking at a reflection on the side of a bubble. He fixes his gaze on the odometer—the digits come into focus, waiting to track his next move.

James sits on the other side of the cab, arms folded, his father's hat between them.

The rain becomes rivulets on the windshield, and the windows start to fog.

"Mommy was very sick when she died. You were three. It was cancer."

"Why should I even listen to you? Why? Why? Why?" James pokes on the radio, spinning the volume to high. The music is loud. "I can't even change any of it!"

Startled, Reggie flips off the radio again and starts the truck. The wiper blades carve water off the windshield. *Thwick, Thwack, Thwick, Thwack.* And they see her out there, under her umbrella, moving their way.

"Carol?"

"It's Mrs. Redding. I left my backpack."

"Right, right. See, we're all going to chip in."

Reggie lowers the window, and Mrs. Redding hands James his bag.

"See you tomorrow, buddy."

"Okay. Bye."

Reggie pulls out of the lot and onto the road.

"I know you've got questions. Give me some time, son, and I'll answer them. Every single one."

The rain is heavier now. The truck climbs the hill in front of the school, sending pinwheels of water from the tires. Reggie knows that James will fall asleep. James can never stay awake driving in the rain.

# TAKING FLIGHT
## *— Harvey Mitro —*
### NON-FICTION

MANGLED CORN stalks are strewn among the striated tracks of mounded dirt, which flow imperfectly east from the borders of the trail. Remnants left from the harvest plough, the strips span out over the barren terrain of the rolling fields, giving my running path an aura of desolation.

My days are equally bleak as lonely hours are spent in the library preparing for end-of-term exams. This academic protocol feels like a plea to some higher power to grant grades that somehow validate my worth as a human being. Meanwhile, the greater energies of my humanity remain unrecognized, holding no value in the educational realm.

I choose to run as an escape, to break from the shadowed thoughts that currently define and confine me. Thus far, the run has granted no solace. Short days have ushered in the cold. Leaves have abandoned the maple forest. The bright sun, which elevated this dreary setting moments ago, now casts mirthless silhouettes as it plunges.

The trail is dark-rutted dirt, edged by sparsely grassed turf, which tumbles at intervals into a denser composition that has been flattened like thick burlap. It snakes along the western edge of the farm field, guided roughly by a stream that connects two crude and muddy offerings.

The first is Columbia Lake, now four-hundred meters behind me, and the other is a shallow floodplain called the Laurel Creek Reservoir in a conservation area about a kilometre ahead. The rhythmic thrust of my stride has whisked me along through the busy University streets, over the green fields of Waterloo's north campus, and onto this path. My hope is that the run and the trail will lead me somewhere else. Somewhere better.

A synergy emerges, like a dialogue between the land and my body. It is an exchange of vitality, natural and familiar. The stream cuts directly through a forest of bare maples, and I lean away to follow the path as it curves to skirt around it. The uneven terrain greets my footfall in a symbiotic dance, and the pace quickens in response. My escape is beginning.

With the sun low to my back, I reach the conservation area. Much of the park is a swamp, though in the drier seasons, forested trails surrounding the reservoir firm up and are lovely for running. Today's mid-December frost has encrusted the ground, opening the trails for a rare visit. Heading north atop an access road on the east side of the reservoir, I can see the entire landscape. Grey-brown, extending west for a half-mile, the water is about two hundred meters wide and pierced throughout by the eerie, spiked spires of dead trees, likely killed off by the flooding of the man-made basin.

Despite its haunting presentation, the water teems with life as hundreds of Canada geese have gathered to organize for the great flight south. Their undeniable majesty opposes the grim surroundings. They have elongated silky necks, jet-black to the crown, save for a white oval swath reaching cheek-to-cheek like a chinstrap. Standing three feet in height with a five-foot wingspan, they are impressively large. This, combined with the multi-hued grey layering of their wings, make them one of the most striking water birds. The noise on the reservoir is astonishing, a honking melee as the geese fraternize. Some dunk their heads in search of food, leaving only their tail-ends to protrude, resembling white tufted pylons on the surface of the water. They invert entirely, long necks extended down in order to rake the silted floor with their beaks. Others seem to be organizing themselves, prepping the formations to be held during flight. I cross over the lock, which runs under the access road and controls the water flow into the stream that guided me here. A sharp cut left takes me off the road onto a flat expanse of tightly cropped grass, which traverses the north side of the reservoir. It is a golf-green because the geese have manicured it with weeks of grazing.

    I run with swift fluidity, powering forward to get through the three miles of trails before dark. It is the venting of an energy left dormant all day during motionless study, and it flows out of me like an emancipation.

    Just then, a drumroll of frantic pattering and loud trumpeting draws my gaze left. They shift together like a horizontal avalanche on the water. A flock, forty or more move beside me with wings wide, webbed feet slapping down awkwardly, running atop the surface of the water, hollering all the way. I am above them on the bank, just ahead of the leader, whose staggered troops file behind with a remarkable economy of space. The ground separating us is a thin white strip of sandy beach, sloping down to the water. Lifting, the geese shed the turmoil of take-off, as if breaking free from chains. The moment becomes at once breathtakingly beautiful, as the critical velocity of the flock morphs chaos into exquisite elegance. They rise, the white layer of sand contrasting the dark water just below them, as distant trees texture the flock with vertical stripes, illuminated by the fiery backlight of the setting sun. Meeting my level gaze, they are only fifteen meters off, matching and surpassing my speed effortlessly. Incrementally higher, the flock drifts toward me fearlessly, like an alternate sky shifting overhead, their leader bringing them mere feet above. Individually, they are vast, with beating wings which give tactile waves and a 'whooshing' sound, amid a spirited conversation of honks that I can feel as much as hear when air rushes from their throats. They angle past, one by one, and I alter my trajectory to run with them. For precious seconds I join their group, grasping the elation of this experience, sprinting with futility to hold on. Climbing still, they leave. The trailing members call out a final farewell from twenty feet above while I stagger to a stop, yearning for more. I watch them glide off over the trees of the nearby wood and out of sight.

Often, when setting my body free on a run, I gain a sense of tranquility. Today was much more and everything has been transformed. What was desolate is magical, what felt forlorn is now glorious. It is a joy to run.

# COLD
## — *Jordan Ryder* —
### FICTION

THE SNOW crunched, the icy crust cracking beneath my boots. The air was so cold I could feel the inside of my nose all the way up my nostrils and down the back of my tongue.

The tracks from the week before were almost buried. My boots found the dip between the edges of the tires, staying between them, careful not to knock the walls of snow on either side. There were two sets: the in, then the out.

I could still hear the crackle the fire had made long after you'd left. The silence when it had gone cold: the embers fading from white to grey to black. In the space of a breath. In the space of a year. I don't remember sitting there; just the colours of the shifting fire as it died, the green glare of the clock: *2:47 a.m.*

Six weeks.

Everything. Nothing, in the end.

It had been nothing in the beginning: a few too many drinks. An apple martini because I'd never had one before. Exams were done, what the hell? You'd been a guy at the bar ordering your drink, laughing when you saw mine. When I'd refused to tell you my name you'd called me Apple Martini, then you'd ordered one for yourself and another for me.

The next morning you'd driven me home in your pickup. It had happened again the next weekend, and the weekend after that.

You were nice. You were easy. You called me Apple Martini.

We laughed. We slept. We fooled around, too. It was easy, and winter break, and most of our friends were gone. I'd travelled home for a week, for Christmas. And then I'd missed my period.

I didn't know your last name then. I'm not sure you knew my first.

Nothing had become everything had become nothing again.

Six weeks.

But of course you knew my name, you'd laughed at the Starbucks cup that said *Janice*. That morning after the six tequila shots and four vodka-crans on the two-for-one special, you'd suggested breakfast. I'd said I couldn't eat. Coffee then. Something. I'd agreed. Then you'd laughed when you saw how they'd misheard my name, and we'd made *Friends* jokes until you dropped me off at my apartment. Three days later I'd started my 'period week' pills.

We hadn't gone out that weekend. You'd texted. Then again, a few days later. By then I knew. By then I didn't want to talk to you.

I had two and a half years left of school. Then grad school, if I was lucky. If my grades held. If the placement went through, then the supervised project. If the thesis went well, and the application interviews. Two and a half years left to get my *first* degree. But nobody did anything with an English undergraduate diploma. Not if I wanted to be a professor. Not if I wanted to write articles that anybody would read, and funding for my research.

The snow crackled under my boots. I'd made it to the end of the laneway. Where it bent, that is. I looked down the road, the one that led to town. The white bank running on either side was flat and unmarked until the road turned again, bending out of sight.

I stopped with my feet in the tire tracks, wondering how long it would take me to walk to the highway. How long it would take me to get back. My fingertips were already numb in my pockets.

I stepped off the tire track to the left, treading as carefully. In a few moments I was at the lake.

The trees swayed beside me, snow drifting down through the branches.

You'd texted. Then you'd stopped texting.

The ice cracked. The wind skating over the flat, swirling white mist up in spins and whirls.

I'd called you when I made the appointment. You were going to drive.

I'd called you when I didn't need it anymore.

Lake water soaked up through the snow, caking in slushy blue chunks, the ice dark underneath. My steps sloshed, the first of the frigid water touching my toes through my socks.

You'd asked if there was anything you could do, so I'd had you drive me to my parents' cabin. They were fair-weather cottagers and wouldn't be back till spring.

I didn't think you'd stay.

I sat on a small bank of snow the wind had made in the middle of the lake. The cold seeped through the fabric of my jeans, freezing my skin under my legs, along my bottom. I remembered the cramps. I remembered the rush, the warmth. I'd spent hours and hours on the toilet. It was after the bleeding had stopped, after the clenching in my gut had loosened, long after I'd gone cold, that I'd called you.

The fire you'd made had crackled, popping in my ears. Standing in the middle of my parents' living room, the red glare flickering and beating in the air behind you. The heat leaking towards me, into my clothes and inside my skin.

It's happening to me too, you'd said.

My hand on my stomach, I'd asked if it was.

# LADY MACBETH
## *— Yelibert Cruz —*
### POETRY

Tonight I heave the wreckage of your vanity
on the necks and hearts over inches and miles of searing ends
for the last time.
Fingertips shake over angels, erasing everything that cries.
Opium anklets chain the fairy tale
you promised me centuries ago.
I never considered you to be the fibbing type,
dirt seeding under your tongue: can I ever just lay under the stars
minus you bringing me a battle? My name never trespasses.
"Count my blessings," you spit, righteousness thrusting
a battle axe to my neck.

Down on my knees
I opened a portal to the dark – your game has taken my spirit,
made me unlearn the power of my sex,
dragged me here, a place under landfills
where murder frowns and makes me the creature
my own father took to the grave.
Tonight everything will open – fears that you lulled to sleep
open their fearsome eyes and drain your blood.
Rest no more, for your cries and grunts
will never will my tresses of lady.
My name and kin no longer will be entrusted to his majesty's
    command.

Know my face, babe, and look as I drown Lady Macbeth.
I strip off the pertinence of your name and power,
the actions that your family crest have seared
and printed against my skin.
No saint or mage will come to your rescue,

my anger is a Morse code that
burns,
stabs,
heats your neck.
No, my crown must collapse under the crass weight of my immortal
    beauty.
One whose validity rests not in the ramblings
of a man that understands everything of wars and hell
but absolutely no knowledge of the game.

Yesterday's fickle lips landed in poison,
your rancid trapdoors ended, needles forcing you to your knees.
"Please," you'll cry, "please have mercy,
mercy of beasts and women."
The women you throw aside for ego, fickle and frail, deserve your
    cut hands.

We breathe for it!
I will come to you as a woman that's bared an astounding curse,
to have her hand given and taken by a man
that yelps for mercy in blood and knives.
Fire will cover your organs all, your murd'ring majestries
have never been so wilted and sad.
Tears will fall, water and the hearth will rise on every moon from within:
your sight will lend me eyes,
your smell will be my smell,
your clubs will stand counter to you.
Please, you'll wail, under tonnes of hate this creature's mane will rise,
captain of your ship and ember to your fear.

Call on me again, Thane, for my tricks of the night,
and you will pay a torturous spell.
Take heed in this warning, Macbeth,
do not underestimate the nest I have conspired of your malice.
One's eyes must keep open for hell,
and when that gate opens

my kingdom will be seen,
my knife will plunder until you're seeping
a knot of crimson through the tears.

Warriors and underlings come to my tits with mangy hands,
knights seeing what pleases and taking.
Oh, never will you thrust your hands, I am eager to my vengeance
    and far too proud.
You creep this song, remember the music,
the grey dagger I hold will be tossed in
the black, unforgiving forest.
Keep your tongue, for I thrive on the delicacy of your pleas.
Ringleaders and knights alike fall tonight,
and you will cry my name.

"Please,"

your heart will pound, life draining, handless, powerless, dying.

"Please!"

# ROMANTIC CANADA
## *— Mark Halpern —*
### FICTION

SOMEWHERE IN Tokyo at the very moment this story begins—most likely—two gentlemen, possibly more, are engaged in argument. The point of contention is whether Toronto, or whether Calgary, is the World's Most Romantic City.

Inspirational leader of those favouring Toronto is Marc. He had lived only in Paris until his posting to Toronto at age twenty-six. Soon after arrival he attended a gathering held by a European business association at an opulent suburban home. There, he fell in love-at-first-sight with Yvette, also from Paris, also twenty-six. When the gathering ended, nothing was open nearby except a Mister Donut shop. So that is where they went, and where—according to Marc—Yvette in turn, fell in love with him. As they melted into each other's eyes—again, according to Marc—they were sharing an unusual type of donut they later learned bore the appellation, "French Cruller." This Marc chose to interpret as a sign of fate.

Leading the side for Calgary is Jiro, who originally hailed from Kyoto. His father wrote biting social commentary and secretly, under a pen name, a highly popular series of novels that, because of his artistry, were termed "erotica" rather than "unrelentingly gross and offensive pornography." He eventually confessed—only to Jiro—the actual source of the family's principal income, noting, "to write imaginative but credible smut, one needs creativity, relevant life experience, and facility with a tape measure, protractor, and stop watch."

Jiro was pushed to study literature and history, but pushed himself in other directions. He became fully fluent in English, even better at math, and better still at science and technology. Upon entering the engineering faculty at Kyoto University, he joined its American football team, the Gangsters, earning the nickname "Crusher." Jiro's mother, an eleventh-generation tea ceremony master, could not quite understand how she had produced such a child.

At age twenty, Jiro took a summer course in Calgary. During a visit to its famous Stampede he met Jenny, an earthy, auburn-haired beauty. She was his first and only true love. Jenny felt differently toward Jiro, and the relationship did not survive the summer. But Jiro has his memories.*

\* \* \*

Our brief, indeterminate story proper begins with young Eric Peabody disembarking an Airbus 380 at Haneda Airport—ignorant of the possibility anyone anywhere might regard any city in English Canada as noteworthily romantic. That ignorance had not disturbed his consistent happiness, which flowed ultimately from an unprideful, optimistic recognition of his own fine and decent character.

It was love that brought Eric to Tokyo. First, a passionate adoration of big cities propelled him away from his childhood Calgary and towards University of Toronto. Upon graduation, a tender infatuation with things Japanese brought inspiration; with love's light wings did he thus o'erperch other job offers, into the mechanical arms of auto-parts maker, ShinNaka Canada. Eric's romance with superior-quality auto parts blossomed and he will presently commence a training program at ShinNaka's Tokyo headquarters. A long-ish sojourn. In three months he would return to the familiar.

But three months is as short-ish as it is long-ish. Straight to the dormitory and onto his tiny balcony-for-one, Eric gazed toward the evening dazzle of central Tokyo. For all he knew, he was staring right at the ShinNaka Building, where he would report for duty thirty-six hours later.

Jet lag permitted but little sleep and mandated much subsequent half-awakeness. At dawn, Eric propelled himself all the way to Kamakura, even before its solemnly-mystical Zen temples opened. From amidst the early-Sunday barrenness, an expensively-dressed fiftyish woman approached. She held a sign, "Free Tour—English or German." After demanding his nationality, she produced a Canadian flag on an extendable rod, promising to wave it high should they "become separated in the crowd." Such was her efficiency that the magnificently data-intensive tour, including the Giant Buddha, was over in two hours. But no time to wait for a gift, or even a full expression of Eric's gratitude. She remained "on duty." As he looked back from the now-crowded station, she triumphantly hoisted a Lichtenstein flag, having beaten heavy competition from other sign-bearing women.

Soon Eric was wandering through postwar Tokyo—as recreated within the Shin-Yokohama Ramen Museum—sampling the wares of 1950s-style noodle shops. Next, a "clone factory," followed by photographs with Anpan Man, an edible superhero, and some of his toddler fans. Then one bath after another at a hot-spring complex. Then el-cheapo sushi, tastier than the expensive stuff back home. A calligraphy museum; a toilet museum; a multilingual robot bartender serving pints. Later, dried squid was vended by a machine to vanquish midnight dormitory peckishness. Eric, head on his pillow, tried to rank-order the day's weirdnesses, but gave up.

\* \* \*

Back momentarily to Marc. Now Asia Pacific head for a major multinational, he lives in Tokyo with still-adored Yvette and their two flawless children. A born leader, bon vivant and byword for elegance, Marc spent twenty-four years developing international markets for luxury brands. But he is, also, a practical man, credited with extending formerly-glittering logos into selected regional markets for shoe inserts, pet diapers, and kitchen-grease absorption pads. Marc has come to know the world's great cities intimately. To him, Toronto still rules.

As for Jiro, he joined a large auto manufacturer and worked very, very hard. Everyone saw his potential to go right to the top, with his rough-and-ready charm, cold logic, strategic-mindedness and tightly self-controlled passion for life. It was during postings overseas that Jiro most deeply craved someone to love and to love him back. Though married with children and copiously befriended, he was alone. We find him too in Tokyo, his career still flying skyward, his heart still tied down.

\* \* \*

Eric surrendered his expectations and relaxed into his designated seat at the trainees' welcome party, next to the veteran employee assigned as their mentor. The latter had years earlier fallen under the influence of Jiro, whose company was ShinNaka's biggest customer.

The personnel files indicated Eric's birthplace. From this, the mentor's mind had formed an image of a cowboy romping through prairie flowers surrounding a towering oil well, the rusty-red sun reflecting back from adjacent glass-and-steel skyscrapers. In person, Eric fit the image well enough—tall and broad-shouldered, sandy-haired good looks, a healthy appetite for beer. Upon inquiry, he revealed that he could ride a horse.

Several pints later, the mentor asked about good spots to someday visit in Calgary. Eric mentioned Lake Louise and Banff, but the mentor pressed for recommendations within Calgary proper. He said it must surely be filled with beauty and grace, given its reputation as the World's Most Romantic City. By good fortune, another trainee distracted him from viewing approximately 40ml of beer foam emerge from the nostrils of Eric, who regarded the remark as clever irony—beyond what had seemed possible for a Japanese person speaking English.

Oblivious to the frothing's residue, the mentor invited Eric to an upcoming networking event sponsored by local and foreign business associations.

\* \* \*

This was just the sort of event where, on rare occasions, Marc and Jiro might actually meet. And even, perhaps, do good-natured battle before the assembled crowd, as if to vindicate the relative honour of patron-goddesses of competing city-states.

But the Argument was not confined to these two champions. Each, by virtue of strength of personality—such virtue, like all virtues, amplified by its exemplar's position in society— managed to recruit to his cause a coterie of businessmen and salarymen. These disciples (and their sub-disciples) were ready at all times to argue fervently in favour of the romantic-ness of Toronto or Calgary, as the case may be. And given how powerfully Marc and Jiro desired affirmation of their respective convictions, the numbers recruited were rather large.

Hundreds, at least, on each side.

There were no pre-arranged set-piece battles. But the Argument sprung to life almost whenever members of the Toronto and Calgary factions happened to meet. Accordingly, given their numbers and that they moved in overlapping social and business circles, one may confidently assert that the Argument was most likely underway somewhere in Tokyo constantly from noon to ten-thirty p.m. During the timespan relevant to this story.

Note also that the number of factioneers is particularly astonishing when one considers that few had made more than a single one-night trip, if even that, to either Toronto or Calgary. And often it was the "wrong" city. Thus, one might speculate that their professed strong opinions are *tatemae* (sometimes described as an outward façade, but which might be understood as a species of truth emanating from one's position in all social groupings relevant to a particular occasion) rather than *honne* (an inner truth of deep-down feelings). But that hardly matters.

One might further speculate that all this advocacy of one faraway city or another sprang from desires unrelated to Canada or even to romance. The desire to experience the comforts of membership in yet another well-defined group. The desire to have, at the ready, a portfolio of things to say at social gatherings, with some scope for originality within the constraints of a pre-determined over-arching group opinion. The desire, perhaps most of all, to feel connection with a great and charismatic personality—the rare nail that stands up in Japan, but no one wishes to bang down. But, again, that hardly matters.

Marc and Jiro surely knew all this. Yet each, compelled by his heart, persisted in the active idealization of a specific Canadian municipality. One celebrating joyously, the other reaching out for catharsis.

\* \* \*

Though the factions had defied formalization, occasionally some smarmy devotee, hoping to impress Marc or Jiro, would make an attempt. Thus, as Eric arrived at the networking event, someone was selectively handing out t-shirts bearing Calgary's rousing civic motto, "Onward." It occurred to no one that Toronto's motto, "Diversity Our Strength," better illustrates the English un-grammar typically adorning Japanese casual wear.

After ensuring Eric received a t-shirt, the mentor sought out co-factioneers. Chuffed with pride, he introduced his protégé. His real-live Calgarian with firsthand knowledge of Toronto—who might replenish their spent ammunition. How it is that Eric twigged on is unclear. Perhaps his mind had sharpened through the many hours of training, study, and social activities hyper-organized by ShinNaka. Perhaps Eric's initial Tokyo experiences had primed him for open-mindedness. Regardless, he discoursed spiritedly upon Calgary's merits, especially its alluring women; his restraint in denigrating Toronto was interpreted as good manners.

Once left to mingle at will, Eric cast about for a fellow Canadian who might offer intelligible insight into the lay of the land. He fell into conversation with a Quebecois recently employed by a French bank. The latter invited Eric to a second party afterwards, apologizing that some conversation would be in French. *Pas de problème*, responded Eric. They hit it off instantly, the way one cannot often do after turning thirty.

The main event neared its close and Eric found his way back to the mentor, who stood at the periphery of a swirling, dark-suited vortex of t-shirt-clutching men. The mentor tugged him toward its mighty focal point, where Jiro thrust out his hand. "Howdy, pardner," he boomed. "Put 'er there." He slapped Eric's back and they exchanged business cards. Before directing his attention elsewhere, Jiro said he would be in touch soon.

After adequate goodbyes, Eric made his way to an upscale *izakaya*, sliding into an empty seat at the end of a long table populated by a half-dozen elegantly-attired Western men and equal number of exquisitely-silken Japanese women. The men were competing in clever conversation, those sitting nearest in French. Eric participated passably well. Suddenly, Marc, his silver hair set off by his midnight-blue suit, made an entrance, which, owing to substantial drinking beforehand, was exceptionally grand. Waves of splendour emanated outward. No one in the joint could keep their eyes off him.

He sat down next to Eric and was promptly moved to tears at the mere realization he was conversing *en français* in Tokyo *avec quelqu'un* from Toronto. Toronto, oh Toronto. Even its donut shops—of which there are veritably many—have a romantic character of the *je-ne-sais-quoi* variety. Marc's mood was not impaired even when, upon prodding, he conceded that he had not, for purposes of comparison or otherwise, deigned to investigate the donut shops of other cities.

Eric, well practiced at metabolizing alcohol, kept his wits while others sank towards obliteration. The less-serious drinkers departed—one with Eric's new t-shirt wrapped around his head like a bandana. When closing time came, Eric was surprised to learn that the trains had already stopped running and accepted a lift from Marc, whose chauffeur awaited. During the forty-minute ride, Marc opened his heart as if young Eric were among his dearest friends. Most probably this was a function of not merely the drink nor even the release from a stressful work day, but also a perception of Eric's solidity: Eric was a straight arrow. Toronto and Calgary may also have been factors.

\* \* \*

Eric would have been thoroughly contented even had his next eleven weeks comprised only ShinNaka responsibilities punctuated by explorations of Tokyo. But Marc added good companionship and good career advice, and, moreover, introductions to a mind-boggling number of gorgeous women. Although none inspired feelings of love, they did, collectively, cement Eric's commitment to Japan.

Meanwhile, he was favoured by Jiro with invitations to industry events and social gatherings, at which Eric played his expected role with skill and enthusiasm. At the barbecue on his final weekend, he turned up sporting a Stetson, purchased in Ginza, believing—*tatemae*tically—everything he said about romantic Canada. Eric presented to Jiro, as to Marc, a youthful sincerity each older man wanted to keep discovering in himself.

Jiro extended invitations equally to the mentor, whose estimation of Eric grew and grew, culminating in ShinNaka's highest-ever formal trainee evaluation.

\* \* \*

Four years of hard work and dedicated language study. Then Eric transferred to Tokyo as ShinNaka's youngest-ever inbound employee on an expat remuneration package.

Marc was back in Europe, heading up global marketing, and seldom visited Japan. Jiro was still there, but now as Senior Executive Vice President his days and evenings were taken up with electric vehicle development, strategic acquisitions and avoiding corporate scandals. Neither Marc nor Jiro had much time for self-indulgent reminiscing, though it is unclear whether they had matured or merely grown older. What was undeniable was that without their active presence on the Tokyo social scene, the Toronto and Calgary factions, both tenuously grounded from the start, had faded to nothingness.

Eric embraced Japan. He had arrived, as before, without aims beyond experiencing life and learning therefrom. Through this, he built a fine career in the auto parts business and a good number of lasting friendships. As for romance, there were several iterations of bliss, but he also spent much time crying into his sake. As our story comes to an end, Eric felt very close to a young woman named Harumi. I am not privy to the details. I can only say that he eventually came to regard Tokyo as the World's Most Romantic City.

# HIS FARM
## *Sarah Gardiner*
### FICTION

THE FIRE crackled and hissed. She turned her back to the hellish flame. With tears in her eyes, Dani swallowed the lump, pulled her jacket tight, and released a small shiver. For all the heat surrounding her, her body remained cold. Feeling her husband's strong hand entwined in hers, he gave a supportive squeeze as they walked towards the house.

It was strange how she could still love the house. Impressively tall, solid like a mountain. It was hard to tell in the dark, but the house itself was all stone in shades of blues and greys. The white shutters used to bang horrifically in storms. With golden flowing ease, the surrounding canola fields provided a stark contrast next to the sturdy home. He had loved his farm. Using such tenderness to care for the crops, the equipment, the house, and the dog. She hated that dog. That dog was loved and nurtured.

Their shoes now crunched and kicked against the pebbled path. Dani remembered the week he laid down these rocks. Wheelbarrow after wheelbarrow, unloading and loading, shovelling and raking, until the final day at dusk when a perfectly level trail curved up to the house and surrounded the wrap-around porch.

They reached the house and sat on the front steps, watching as orange embers peppered the night sky. The fire seemed to make the fields glow, as if presenting all that was now hers. After all he had taken from her, she now owned everything that he'd taken it for.

Since arriving, not a word had been spoken between Dani and her husband. He knew what needed to be done, and she was grateful for that. Driving up the dirt road, she didn't recognize any turns or steep hills, dusting up the truck as they pummelled down the next. She had lived in this house for sixteen years, and had been driven down that road exactly nine times. The first few times she was too young to remember. It was shortly after her mother had died and he hadn't a clue what to do with a baby. After he hired Molly though, there were only four times Dani had left the property.

One morning, when Dani was six years old, she woke up covered in spots. Frantic with paranoia, as if she had the plague, he had thrown her into his pickup truck and driven her straight to some hospital. Dani had never seen a hospital, or another building for that matter. He left her there for four days. Every day after that, until the day she escaped, she dreamed of that mechanical bed with the soft pillow. The smiling nurses would bring her warm chocolate pudding. When the itching had subsided she remembered sitting up in that bed, hands pressed together, praying for more painful sores to come—they never did.

The second time was when Dani was thirteen. The screams could be heard from the barns and beyond. Bolting up the stairs, he had been covered in oil and dirt, likely working on one of the tractors. Molly had followed, her apron also covered in dirt. She had been digging potatoes for dinner. There was Dani, perched on the toilet with blood covered hands and terrified eyes as gaped as her mouth. Dani remembered his reaction being quite unexpected. He wasn't mad, he didn't yell, he didn't hit. He had slid down the wall, face in hands, as if in defeat. Something had changed, she didn't know what. Molly drove her to town to get new pants and white puffy pads. He had wanted Dani out of his sight.

The third time was when she was fifteen. She was mad and wanted to defy him. Dani climbed as high as she could, branches scratching her arms, thick leaves brushed against her face. She jumped from the apple tree by the old wood barn and broke her leg. She got to have pudding again.

Her final drive down that dirt road has never been talked about.

No matter how cold and frightening the bedroom was, the rest of the house was always warm and safe. Rolling pie dough with Molly, picking herbs in the garden, playing cards around the hearth—she cherished those moments. They made the nights bearable when she would close her eyes, let her body go, and drift away. Images would appear of the morning sun with steaming tea and warm bread. The barn cats would scamper and play in the red wagon. Her and Molly sipping soup on the covered porch while it rained. When it was over and he'd leave, her mind would clear. She didn't just cherish those memories, the memories protected her.

The sky began to darken again as the fire calmed. Gesturing to her husband to stay put, Dani walked down the steps and opened the tailgate to the truck. She pulled out the sign and carried it down the path. Reaching the post she looked back at the house. How strange to see such a good man sitting on those steps. She hung the sign on the hooks and walked back.

A squeaky creak came from behind them. "Ready to go?" Molly pushed through the screen door. She pulled the key from her pocket and turned the bolt.

Dani looked over her shoulder and nodded at her friend. Molly was the mother she never knew. Her only true family. And in the end, the woman who saved her.

On the steps of her childhood stood the only reasons for Dani to push through. A man who knew very little about this place, and a woman who knew it all. Molly reached for Dani's face and brushed a tear from her cheek.

They drove away, past the house and past the barns, then onto the dirt road. The sky was once again dark, the fire behind them had dwindled down to smouldering ash.

What remained of the bed would be black, cold, and dead by morning.

# LUPÉ, A DENTRO DEL METRO
## — *Hanorah Hanley* —
### POETRY

i stare through the blue, blue chair across from me
until it grows, and
swallows all the bits of me
and i,
just a pair of eyes.

Still, it does not erase Her from my view.

She is a mystic.
Yellow, all in yellow: hat, jacket, scarf.
She burns my eyes.

She wove a novel of her pain and mailed it to my mind.
i made a mosaic of the remains,
i shaped the shards,
But She,
She built the vase.

A low E rumbles. The doors open. Her nose turns.

i count the crushed cockroaches under my shoe.
i sing the Second-Wife Blues.

# SOMNIFICANCE
## — *Sheri Falconer* —
### FICTION

THE SMALL bird hit the window with a smack. It probably died instantly, a broken neck. Katrina rushed to snatch up the sparrow before Bailey could grab it. The dog had a penchant for dead things. Pulling on gardening gloves, she grabbed a shovel, scooped the broken bird, and marched to the edge of her garden. Bailey joined in the procession, wagging his tail. As she buried the bird, Bailey spotted a squirrel and ran after it. Katrina returned to moving boxes from the boat to the porch.

The stuffed fish mounted over the fireplace was her father's edition to the décor. A banal detail in a hunting cabin, but maybe a mandatory one. Every year, as they opened the cottage, her father would recount the hard-fought battle to reel in his prized pike.

When she was five, she asked her Dad, "Do fish have eyelids?"

Her father, so large in that moment, answered, "They don't need em, when you're underwater, your eyes don't dry out."

Ghosts, she was going to lodge with ghosts all winter.

As she ran the feather duster along its faded scales, she could hear his voice. Her father wiped down Blinky's scales right along with her. Blinky just stared with an empty wide-eyed gaze. What a stupid name for a fish, but it left Katrina tearing up.

Sweeping down rough walls, chasing out spiders and dust, Katrina carried on cleaning. She pulled the dust covers from the furniture and folded them. Kind of like removing vestiges of an old life, like shaking out the curtains. This space was solely hers to redecorate later.

A mishmash of furniture hand-me-downs gave the room a far-flung eclectic look. The love seat, a threadbare red plaid, was the sole survivor of a three-piece set from Aunt Marg's house. Aunt Marg became a Steinman when she married Uncle Fred. They were gone too, leaving Katrina, the last in the line of Wainwrights.

As Katrina began to unpack boxes, she still hadn't come across the coffee grounds. She wouldn't make it a week, not without caffeine. It was in the second last box. As she set a can on the counter, there was a scurrying of tiny feet through the cupboards below. Katrina was housemates with a whole community of mice. She should adopt a cat. She smiled. David hated cats.

There was a time, she'd imagined a boy with David's golden curls and sometimes with her hazel eyes, definitely not her nose. Her father would have swung a puffy red lifejacket over his head, tying the twill tape ties tight and herded him down to the water just like he'd done with her all those years ago. They'd float out in his rowboat with a lunch pail full of peanut butter sandwiches, sliding grimy earthworms onto a hook and drop a line in the water. It was never about the fish, Katrina knew that now.

Perhaps she and David might have made it with a child. 'But babies don't work well to patch what needs mended. Truth be told, it only tears holes bigger with the strain.' Her mother whispered in her memories.

All the hustling and sweating just to sink into a Muskoka chair at the end of the dock with a coffee. At least that was the way Katrina pictured it all those years ago while she put in long hours to pay for a city escape. One more client. One more payment to purchase solitude. David never stayed long when he came, didn't care for still life in primitive. Forget the wild fauvist colour of a sunset.

Bears, or was it Bulls, can gore away the better part of a life's work in one run of the market. It had been a mistake to leave business to David. His moods rose with tidal crests and sank with its fall. Reading signs and omens between lines on newsprint loaded with a powder keg of pomp and spectacle. As David's realm crumbled when the recession hit, he sought out long shot stocks even harder to recover his loss. That was when Katrina really lost him.

Outside under the stars it was so clear.

No point wishing for what could have been. Bailey scratched at the door. Katrina threw on her coat, heading out the door after Bailey into the twilight.

Katrina threw a stick for Bailey to fetch. He splashed into the lake, breaking up the reflected sky. A crisp clear sky spilled over with ink and peppered with stars while she had cleaned. A vast expanse of nothingness made visible with the disappearance of the sun.

'Got to rest sometime,' she heard her dad say. 'Halley's comet only comes into view every three-quarters of a century. Get your nose out of that book and come outside a spell and marvel at the universe.'

She watched her breath puff into clouds.

Her phone lay silent on the desk inside. Nothing pressing anyways. Well, she longed for silence. Now she had it. One hundred calls a day tending towards insanity down to none.

Mosquitos buzzed about her ears. A constant rush of the wind through the cedars joined with the pounding of her pulse in her ears. Both steady, somnolent, and significant as autumn's exit. A world tending towards sleep, time enough for it.

Bailey pushed his soft head into her hands. Katrina ruffled his ears. Bailey nudged in closer.

In the absence of city light, the stars glowed like beacons, the milky way a dense spattering spill dividing the black ink of the sky. Katrina could almost imagine them being poured out, their light streaming towards the earth. Hoary hosts shining and spiralling like Vincent Van Gogh's *Starry Night* with a consoling crescent moon overhead.

A slice of the heavens painted in an asylum, Van Gogh sketched studies of the sky from his own wilderness of sorts.

Things seen in the heavens, stars, distant swirling galaxies, already spent and burnt out like her efforts to reach this same point, days, months and years ago. Reaching earth, a picture of what was, like the photo of her and David on her nightstand. Old light from moments before. Who knew if they were still shining somewhere up there now? Uncertainty being certain in almost every sphere. To walk abreast another a blessing no matter how brief, for you weren't walking alone. You never know how close you step towards the threshold to eternity.

A meteor shower sprinkled light across the black sky like sparks. Katrina's hair grew out silver waiting to leave the city. Now here in the void, she wondered if she would last. A tiny corpuscle lost in a vast, wild array.

Small bodies wandering through independent systems, doing their duties until they were needed no more, floating freely through the void, colliding as they will and interacting in predictable ways. Remnants of exploding stars forever falling until they hit bottom. Wildly winging moths flirting with disaster by the porch light.

David was always on a different trajectory than hers. She loved him once, she loved him still. He hadn't reached his pinnacle yet. One day he'd be ready to plummet back to earth. Pity that those who soar the highest often arch back down so sharply to fall the farthest. Part of her wished she'd be there for the spectacle.

It had been a rush to be part of his sphere. The noise, the play by play of economies as titans chose whether they took sugar in their coffee. All the smaller stars emulate those on top.

Katrina took her perfunctory bow and left the room. Her moment had passed.

She read somewhere that the largest star in Van Gogh's painting was actually Venus. A planet named for goddess of love and beauty rotating contrary to the other orbs, rising to face the sun in the west and bedding into darkness in the east. A slow kiss to the waking in passing trajectories. Lovers turn away.

As she stared at the heavens, the only star Katrina could pick out was Polaris, the north star, shining bright like the point of a stellar compass. Sailors navigated by the stars, so did explorers. Katrina knew which way was north.

True north, fixed and unchanging, and then there was magnetic north, ever migrating as the magnetic molten heart of the earth stirred. Her compass point shifted from David. Katrina, explorer of the stars, adjusting her inclinations, searching for her true north.

# SCARBOROUGH
## — *Kelly-Anne Maddox* —
### NON-FICTION

THE THREE of you giggle down the sidewalk, ambling arm in arm past garages and gas stations, used car dealers where you can buy a 1980 station wagon, faded playboy decal in the back window, no money down.

The July heatwave glints off anonymous windshields racing to the next red light on the four-lane parkway as exhaust fumes sting your nose. You play games to see who can blow the biggest bubbles, belt out Def Leppard to air guitar chords and high pitched squeals.

You're fifteen and a fish out of water. You spent the past year scraping up enough money teaching piano lessons to buy a plane ticket to Toronto. Anything to escape the claustrophobic village clinging to the North Atlantic cliffs, even if it's only for two weeks. You're visiting friends, Tina and Tracey, sisters; a childhood ensconced in your little village, doing everything with them. You rode your bikes together, laughed, fought and made up, had sleepovers, spent snow days when school was cancelled building forts, throwing snowballs, and running indoors to warm up.

The bliss of childhood friendship ended when their parents split up and their mother relocated them to Oshawa. There was suddenly a void in your life, and you're trying to fill it with this trip. But you soon learn that they not only had to move provinces away, but that they had to grow up overnight. They're cosmopolitan, worldly, talk of real boys they've made out with, periods, getting their driver's licence.

Things that no one discusses in the village.

And so that day you hop on the bus together—old times in a new place—head to the nearby city of Scarborough to visit their grandmother, the one who left her husband and children marooned in the village way back in the 60s to move to Toronto with her lover.

You walk into the high-rise, the concrete stack camouflaged within a tunnel of apartment towers, laundry dangling from balconies, crisp and shrivelled plants escaping through railings, a hint of curry lingering at the entrances. The skin on your arms prickles from the shock of the air conditioning and your eyes squint to a slit as you go from daylight to dusk.

In the elevator, the smell of burnt out cigarettes and Lysol envelopes you and the first thing you see is the poster. A man, not much older than you, hooded eyes staring you down as you try to look away. Blond hair, swooping cowlick across his forehead, preppy in a private school kind of way. In a different context, he could be cute, could be anybody's older brother, perhaps even one of the celebrities whose images you and your friends plaster on your bedroom walls, fantasize about. *What if Kirk Cameron asked you to marry him? Which of the Coreys do you like best?* In another world, the man in the poster could be any of these were it not for the title in bold print that you just can't avoid: "The Scarborough Rapist."

You've never heard of the Scarborough Rapist but you remember that bad things happen in big cities.

Yet you're not scared. Not then.

It won't be until after high school that you start to connect the dots as one of Canada's most notorious serial killers is caught—a rapist, torturer, murderer of teenage girls the same age as you—and you wonder, could that be him? And then nearly twenty years later, your baby girl asleep on your lap, you read an article about how he honed his skills, targeting young women, following them home from bus stops, attacking them.

In Scarborough.

Finally you're scared. For yourself. For your daughter. For those three girls who thought that nothing could touch them.

# ENLIGHTENMENT
## — *Susan Siddeley* —
POETRY

I'm aware of my knees now
creaking, for no good reason
when I put a hand on the mantel
to rise from a fire lighting or floor scrub
(Not that I do much of either.)

Should I need to pray for inspiration
I gaze heavenwards, conscious of my
neck clicking
Aware of my knuckles
curling, and not just when I hold
an alabaster egg from Combarbala
or a cup of coffee.

Of my head nodding, even though I don't
agree with the agenda. Of my
heart beating at the sight of dawn over the Andes
instead of the butcher's sly grin
as he cleans a roast for me.

Nails are ridged,
with the regularity that would better bless
a guitar keyboard.
Toes all anyhow and skin
mottled as the rock I sit on
staring at my knees
instead of out
over the Pacific.

# A LUNA MOTH
## — *Jennifer Turney* —
### FICTION

IT STARTED with an obituary.
The package that followed, a framed Luna Moth, touched her heart.
The real estate listing sealing the deal.

As Audra neared the end of her six hour drive north of Toronto, her mind was a beehive of activity. Gone were the billboards and streetlights, the hums and honks of heavy traffic. The highway was lined with tackle shops, diners advertising 'Fresh Baked Pies' and 'Pickerel Cheeks'. Rock cuts jutted out on either side with birch trees clinging, defying gravity.

\*\*\*

The crunching gravel of Mallard Lane broke Audra from her asphalt trance. She held her breath heading down a steep hill as she manoeuvred the narrow lane surrounded by thick raspberry bushes whispering against the side mirrors. She turned a corner and the lane ended at a cottage that was the wrong colour. Now sage green, she remembered it bright yellow and affectionately labelled 'The 3 Bears' for the Thiberts Family who had built it.

Audra found the right laneway fifty yards behind, two worn tracks with tufted dry grass between; a chain across halted her progress. She hiked the rest of the way.

The air was so fresh Audra inhaled deeply to savour it. She remembered the deep green balsams bordering the trail and came out from their shady embrace into the yard filled with orange fireweed and yellow buttercups. The bees floated lazily between them; pollen heavy and drunk with sunshine.

The cottage was still red. The shed was still dark green and a quick peek confirmed that the beloved outhouse was still there with its earthy aroma mixed with lye and giant wolf spiders completing the horror.

The screen door creaked as Audra unlocked it.

"Oh, wow," she gasped.

Stepping inside, she was taken back twenty years—the too-big dinner table, the wood-powered stove. The shelves had the same daisy-specked curtains strung instead of doors and the toilet was still crammed in the closet as an afterthought of modern comfort.

She made her way through the room, slowly, reverently, as one would walk through an empty church. Audra's fingers brushed on the harsh fabric of the daybed and the smooth leather of the kitchen chairs, the room perfumed by mosquito coils long-since burned out from countless summers past.

"It may only be one room," Audra said as she pulled back the wall of curtains, revealing Wolf Lake, "but the view definitely makes up for it."

She glanced at the old rotary phone mounted on the wall and the note written in her grandmother's curling script dictating 'party line etiquette'.

"Is that even still a thing?" she wondered out loud to herself.

\* \* \*

Picking up the receiver, she heard people talking and stifled a laugh before hanging up. "I guess so!"

The television with rabbit-ears reminded her of all the patience her grandfather had used trying to angle for a station, and how every program seemed ancient on the black and white screen.

Stepping back outside, she remembered too late to catch the screen door and jumped with a giggle at the SLAM!

She remembered leaping off the dock, swimming, and the slimy weeds that tickled her feet; the memory made her shiver.

She remembered chipmunks eating corn and peanuts from her hand.

Audra wrapped her arms around herself, overwhelmed as details flooded her brain.

*Could this be the place?*

She knew it intimately, quiet and calm like the water lapping on the shore. It would be an adjustment from the life she'd been living in the city. It could be *the* change.

As Audra turned to lock up, she found the sign she needed.

Resting near the porch light was a Luna Moth. The discovery took her breath away; she'd never seen a live one. The framed moth had been preserved by her grandmother. This one also had tiny singes on the tips of its wings, but it was the most beautiful thing she'd ever seen. The green was indescribable.

"That's it then," Audra decided, reassured.

Everything moved quickly once she returned home. Within the week she'd bought her family cottage, and Audra had left her job downtown.

"Are you crazy?" her assistant asked as she packed up her desk.

"I can't explain it," Audra said. "It's something I've been thinking about for a while. I need a change."

"So you're moving to the middle of nowhere?"

"No," Audra said, clutching her box of belongings. "I'm going home."

# GRAPEFRUIT BREAK
## — *Kristin Fast* —
### SHORT PROSE

    I punch my thumbnail through the button-like bottom of the peel, wiggling my nail through the thick depth of it. It tears finally, and my nail nicks the citrus flesh beneath. I work back a section of rind big enough to pull and I tug until it rips away, leaving a healthy layer of pith behind.

    It's tedious work, peeling a grapefruit. It lets go in slow layers.

    I peel the rind piecemeal, piling the peach-coloured strips on a napkin in front of me. Every now and then I take a sip of coffee. Sharp rind residue lingers on my hands, mixing with sweet cream in my mouth. Blue winter sunshine flows through Mac Hall. I settle, anchored to calm in the rush between classes.

    The coloured peel is gone. Time to tackle the pith. It's tough; it clings to the flesh; it hates to yield. Soon I've strewn white curls across three separate napkins, each one soggy where I dried juicy fingers.

    Halfway around I give in. I peel the fruit in half and use my teeth. I suck the flesh away and leave the pith behind.

    You said you'd be meeting me. Or at least, you said you'd try. That try is a slender bridge; it's kept my mind steady. If you don't show—well.

    I unstick a fresh section of grapefruit and slurp it out of its skin. My eyes skitter over the faces in front of me, drawn to upright figures in sagging backpacks. I sip from my cup. I shift slant in my chair.

    The clock in the hall is behind me, but I don't twist to see the time. The crowd has thinned. Ten minutes—a bare ten minutes—and coffee on my tongue makes my mouth pucker.

# I SEE YOU, DO YOU SEE ME?
## — *Desiree Kendricks* —
### FICTION

"YES!" ONE giant leap from the subway platform lands me on the last train car. I swing the backpack off my shoulder, depositing worldly possessions at my feet. *Whoosh!* The train doors close. Wind whistles. I exhale. Grasping the metal pole, my twenty-year-old lanky body jerks with every rumble. Knees bounce. Earbuds snug, skinny jeans tight, bomber jacket loose. Staring at my crimson sneakers I see two months of waiter tips and macaroni and cheese dinners.

I spot you across the aisle. Your moving lips are out of sync with my playlist. I observe your daily complaint, flowing like molten lava, hot angry words cascading. The Barista mangled your name *again*. "Don't they teach kids in school how to spell anymore?" A lip reader I am not, yet I get the message. The train chugs to a stop.

"No!" you exclaim, mouth pouting. Hot liquid tasted by your cashmere coat. Your disappointment soaked up by your companion. A condescending stare appraises my book bag. Our eyes lock. I hear your intake of breath—horrified by the colony of germs socializing on the bottom of my student backpack. You're wondering why for the love of fashion do I spend good money on threadbare jeans; expose my bare knees, show my flattened pockets. You sip your jolt of caffeine, dab at the coffee stain, and yet you question my shopping habits. You're drinking your savings away. You must have shares in coffee beans, given your daily investment.

    Skullcap tugged from my head reveals messy hair. I was in a rush. But it is the neck tattoo that unnerves you. More ink on my body than in my school notebook, you suspect. You're wrong. Yes, I use my laptop for note-taking, itemize lists on my phone, and share documents on Google Drive. I'm the generation reverting to ape behaviours, using our thumbs to punch digits. Yes, we're documenting our life on Instagram. So, maybe I don't hold a pen on a daily basis, but I'm gathering knowledge. Love reading. You likely think I only have the attention span to read one hundred and forty characters at a time. I hear you twitter. Not true. My library is portable. No ink stained fingers, unlike the old man across from me, clutching his newspaper. Doesn't he know he can read on his phone? What? No device? I see a traditionalist—refusing to adapt. Perhaps he confuses scrolling for the art of calligraphy etched parchment, documenting life. He narrows his eyes, glances in my direction. Swipes the lens of his reading glasses in his wool scarf. Something suggests his vision is short-sighted. He doesn't see me. I'm the invisible generation, too busy having fun to rebuild his depleting Canada pension. My heavy backpack, stuffed with medical periodicals and research papers is merely a dirty bag soiled by lack of attention. He fails to see my detailed sewing, where I repaired the ripped zipper, the handy pouch I added to the inside to keep things organized. He assumes I play my music too loud, will need a hearing aid by the time I'm half his age. Yes, I hear him.

    The train crawls to a standstill. An explosion of air inhaled when the doors slide open. Bodies weave, eye contact avoided. The fashionista, with the heeled boot and perfect messy bun, smiles at the toddler in a stroller. A sideways glance reveals the mother's body slumped on a bench seat; a thousand worries sitting in her lap. Catatonic, she stares out the train's window; flashes of grey, white, and black blend together. Bleak outlook painted. Looking up briefly, she zeros in on my reflection in the glass. Have we met before? No. Yet recognition is in the details. I was young once, she muses. Carefree—without responsibilities binding me tight. Idealistic—without reality weighing me down. The rhythmic motion of the train makes her head bob. Her eyes shut, while one hand grasps her child's knee, ensuring safety. Transit lullaby threatens to sedate her, yet she blinks repeatedly. "Yes," she answers the child, kissing the top of his head. I see a protective mama bear and her cub.

Fashionista's gloved hands, locked in prayer, rest on her designer handbag. She sees her future: motherhood. Student loans, car payments, and mortgage offer fertile debt—barren uterus. Her brow dips, head hangs low. Sigh released. Peering up, under false eyelashes, she offers me a close lipped smile. Babbling child grabs her attention. I see the fashionista's thirty-something envy. The sharp head turn, the nonexistent piece of fluff brushed from her skirt. Her gaze falls on the footwear of nearby passengers. Eyes transfixed by my blood red sneakers. I can't tell if she has recognized the brand name or has merely fallen under the trance of the train—viewing without seeing.

Hoisting my backpack, I adjust the frayed shoulder strap and swig a drink from my water bottle. The train shudders, the hypnotic beat creeping to a slowed pulse. *Shush, shush, shush.* Pressing the button, the sliding door releases me from the boxy train car. An overhead ding signals departure. Blurred passengers whizz past me. Yet, I see the elderly man who benefits from my futuristic medical research, my attention to detail woven into his surgical scar. I recognize the tired mother, anxious about her child's health, eager to believe, and willing to put her faith in me. My bedside manner will comfort the fashionista struggling with infertility. As for the coffee patron, who prattles about the kids who can't spell, the younger generation's laziness, and the ugliness of tattoos, she I will treat with patience. Whether it be the third degree burn from her coffee, or cataracts that cloud her sight, or taste buds soured over time, I will listen. My hearing is not impaired. My vision is clear. I see you.

# NIGHTWALKING
## *— Meaghan Hackinen —*
### SHORT PROSE

Just before before University Bridge, sidewalk ice becomes turbid and ridged, mirroring waves on the river below. But it's too cold for waves and I see only an inky sweep, blanketed in ice and snow. Overhead, streetlights pulse like timed lights in a terrarium; a traffic light change initiates a burst of vehicles. As I walk, the peal of engines fades to wind, a snapping rush through the river valley that scrubs the water-resistant material of my hood against the embryonic curve of my ear. Gloved fingers dig for warmth in my pockets; I feel for candy or mints but touch only the jagged silhouette of keys. Upriver, downtown Saskatoon is alight and I recall another landscape, Seymour Mountain at night; me riding a chairlift with freezer-burnt rails, twisting around to see Vancouver flickering electric like pin-holed construction paper held up to the sun. Best on a clear night, when you could gaze past the city to the mouth of the Fraser and into the Valley, and wonder what all those people were doing. In their homes having conversation or shake-n-bake chicken. All those lights. I've never been one to comprehend the scale of things: the cosmos encompasses trillions of stars but the nearest is still farther than I'll ever voyage. There is more saltwater than earth so these masses we call continents are really just islands. I try and imagine those Saskatoon lights as people, one for every human, but it proves impossible so I let them twinkle and blur like phosphorescence in the deep night.

# THE SANDCASTLE
## — *Rosalind Goldsmith* —
### FICTION

HE DIDN'T speak. He held out a handful of mints and offered them to her. She was sitting in the middle of the sandbox with an upside-down pail in front of her and sand islands on her knees and legs. He stood at the edge of the box and waited, holding out the wrapped green candies for her. He was standing for a long time. Finally, she looked up.

"Are those for me?" she said, and wiped her hands on the skirt of her orange dress.

But still he didn't say anything. She got up and stepped towards him. He stretched out his arm a little more to show her that the candies were meant for her. He didn't smile.

She took three and went back to her place in the middle of the sandbox, in front of the upside-down pail. "Come here," she said, "I am building a sandcastle. You can help me."

He stepped into the box, and, putting the rest of the candies in his pocket, sat down beside her. She filled the bucket with damp sand and turned it upside down. "There it is," she said, taking the bucket off, "A sandcastle. You can put something on top of it if you want."

The boy looked at it, picked up a handful of sand and drizzled it on top of the heap. Then with his other hand he flattened the thing.

"That's not nice," she said. "I made that."

He looked at her and stood up. Out of his pocket he took the remaining mints and dropped them into her lap. Then he walked away across the playground to the bench where his mother was waiting for him, book in hand. "Hello, Superman," she said.

He put his hand on her knee and lifted it up and down several times.

"What are you trying to say, Meeps?" she said.

But he just went on lifting his hand up and down on her leg and staring up at her.

"What is it? What's wrong? What happened?" she said, and she bent towards him to lift him up onto the bench. But he insisted on patting her leg over and over, and she thought it must be a new game he was playing, so she began to tap her other knee, copying him, because the therapist told her this can help sometimes, though sometimes not, but it doesn't hurt to try. But the boy pulled her hand away and kept hitting her knee with his hand, harder now, until it almost hurt.

"What's wrong, Meeps? Did someone hit you? Did that little girl hit you?"

He tilted his head, kept hitting her and hitting her, staring at her.

She bent forward, closer to him. "What do you want to tell me?"

He wanted to tell her this: the story of the little girl, the candies, the sandcastle, how he had destroyed it without knowing why–it was not something he wanted to do. But he couldn't say it, couldn't tell it, couldn't even begin to search for the right words, or any words to tell her his story.

And now, in his mind, the story evolved as elaborate and delicate pictures began to bloom: A stone castle, a field of emeralds by a dense forest of majestic trees that swept the rainbow sky with their long graceful fronds. And in the castle grounds, inside a moat of crystalline water, goats and sheep grazed and servants tended to them, carrying wooden buckets of water. And the little girl from the sandbox was there in the castle in a room of her own with rich tapestries of hunters and unicorns on the walls, and she sat in the middle of the room where there was a sandbox, and she was building a beautiful model of the castle she lived in, with turrets and long narrow windows, and a castle keep and she put six little orange flags atop each turret. And in his story now, he was sitting beside her and telling her how he loved her, how beautiful the castle she had built was, and how he would like to live in it with her but could not—not now in any case—as his mother was getting worried. And he quickly memorized all the dimensions of the castle, of each room, of each turret, of each winding staircase. Then he thanked her for being kind to him and gifted her with handfuls of gems he had found in the forest and told her that one day they would meet again, and he would tell her all the secrets of his mind.

Now sounds began to scrape against each other in his head, causing him pain, and there was nothing he could do to keep track of them all, pull them apart, or get them out. And in his frustration, he just kept hitting his mother's leg harder and harder. And then he began to moan.

His mother stood up and took him firmly by the hand. She knew the worst was on its way—she had to get him home. She held his hand tightly and they ran-walked-ran towards the car, where she would pause for a second to call her husband and tell him to get home now, straight away, please.

"It's alright, Meeps," she said as calmly as she could. "We're nearly there." But something like electricity was shooting through her chest as they got to the car, and her head was throbbing as she opened the door.

"It's okay," she said and lifted him in.

But it was not okay. It was never okay. As she settled him into the car seat, she thought of the long, difficult years ahead for her son. How would he manage when she and her husband were gone? How would he manage in five years, in three, in one?

He could not communicate, understood so little, could not reason, and had no emotional life, no imaginative life at all. How could he live on this earth? What kind of a life could he possibly have? She wept, making no noise.

She wiped the tears, smiled into his face and buckled him into the car seat, her fingers fumbling as she tried to close the clasp.

Just then he began to howl.

# THE BUS NORTH
## — *Erin Alladan* —
### POETRY

Trace these highways
Like the lines on your palm.
Run backward and forward
In the grooves of your childhood.
Linger on the bridge and think about
Stepping in rivers twice.
You're getting closer now; you're getting
Farther.

# NO ART
## — *Anna Baines* —
### POETRY

Pick up the pen –
put it down.
Pick it up.
Try to write about it.
Try boiling it down to its essence –
start there and work outward.
Try reading books:
prose written here in this very dwelling,
this place you now find yourself.
Turn their words over in your hands,
put them in your mouth.
Try to study this new shelter:
the drab, soundproof walls.
The way they feel like rising water.
Or listen to the dull, pervasive hum –
try to learn its rhythm.
If you seek its source, you're sure to find it,
feel it in your own rattling ribcage.
What you'll discover, after all this, is:
there is no art here.
Though artists reproduce this place endlessly
across every medium
across centuries,
art cannot live here.
You've heard the term "beautiful pain"
but that beauty comes only as a healing,
a homecoming.
Until then, keep looking
(if it helps you pass the time).
Keep shining lights in the dark corners.

Scream your art into the silence.
When you finally arrive, your art can be born.
You will return
imperceptibly
surprised anyone recognizes you.

# NO ART PT 2. NEIGHBOURS

Dead winter.
Snow banks expand into whiter skies.
A parking lot space at some apartment shows the pavement that
    exists under all this snow.
(It's easy to forget).
This brazen paved space – negative space –
stands starkly, darkly, to the starchy all-engulfing blanket.
It's loud to look at –
and if you look long enough, you'll hear it say:
"I was here for a long time, but I left."
Simple and undeniable, the paved patch is
sharp and unshifting.
What you'll see, if you're looking, is that the car that slept there all
    winter
and never moved
is gone.
Maybe some grand adventure and the gradually shifting weather
called it to dusty mountain roads
or maybe to the coast.
Maybe it's something much more mundane
than the glaring, bellowing strip of concrete suggests.
Or maybe the claws that kept you inside for months have been
    loosened,
even broken.
There's no goodbye note,
no itinerary of travel plans,

no cover story for why
the snow piled so high,
and never touched that hidden space below.
The guarded negative space speaks only the language of leaving.
You've left, moved on.
And I'm happy to see you've left space behind you.

# CANADIAN BIRTHRIGHT
## — *Tamzin Mitchell* —
### NON-FICTION

I KNOW cold. At twenty-four I registered for a New Year's Day polar bear plunge with my father and my brother. I was anorexic and constantly cold, and my mother was afraid the shock of the frigid water would be too much for my heart, but I was nothing if not stubborn. I was half Canadian. Cold made up at least half my birthright.

 I ran into Lake Ontario that year—that anorexic year—in nylon shorts and a spandex spots bra, screaming *ki-yi-yi-yi*. I'd rubber-banded knockoff Crocs to my feet, but they fell off in the water anyway and I didn't know because my feet were so numb. I emerged with one sandal missing and the other flopping sideways from my foot. After, I couldn't find the strength in my limbs to push on my boots. Were my feet still attached? I couldn't tell.

 The cold in Québec City, four years later, is different. Lake Ontario shocked in its sharp, sudden pang of cold—cold *everywhere*—which disappeared into nothing as my skin and everything else lost feeling. Québec City in March is not sharp but bitter, pervasive. I am not roaming the streets in spandex but wearing layer after careful layer. Beneath my jeans, tights hug my legs, and although I wear two gloves on each hand, I tuck my fingers in the fleecy pockets of my down coat. Under my hood, my hat has earflaps. This is a cold for which I am prepared.

The cold of Lake Ontario subsumed me, undid me. This French Canadian cold bites and nips and plays. It tests my resolve: *Is this really what you want to do today?* it asks, wind whipping into my hood and finding the weak spots in my gloves. *Wouldn't you rather be inside?* It is a fickle lover, seducing me and pushing me away, lavishing first attention and then abuse. *Have we met our cold quota?* says my girlfriend. Not yet, I think. I am not cold enough yet.

Québec is a winter wonderland, maybe. Ice is everywhere: thin black sheets coating the sidewalk and thick, opaque blankets covering the marina, blocks of ice entombing outdoor furniture, ton after ton of ice molded with precision into the ice hotel outside the city. Or maybe it is a winter nightmare. At a former prison, now a museum, we step into cells that are dark and dank and grey with age. A centuries-old logbook lists prisoners' names and crimes and nationalities. So many Irish sailors: what must they have thought, landing here where the cold sneaks up and seeks to destroy you? How grim must winter have been, locked in these cells?

But now the prison is comfortably insulated and warmed, and anyway, we need not stay. We step back outside, and the wind wraps us in its embrace. The temperature is rising: it's barely twenty below. My cheeks tingle. I'm as cold as I've been in years, and as satisfied. *Brrr*, whispers my skin. *Brrr*.

# HOMETOWN
## — *Rachel Freeman* —
### POETRY
#### AFTER BOB HICOK'S PRIMER

I remember Stouffville sadly as the place I came from, I existed.
I remember remorsefully, Stouffville, the red neck of Canada.
Turning heads to the right, cricking reluctantly left.
Looking behind them with adoration, to the horizon with fear.
From day break to Sunscreen, I lived in Stouffville.
18 years.
18 formative years.

The Provincial bird is a honey bee.
Making things sticky and sweet but they can still sting.
The Provincial flower is the church steeple, which sounds holier
    than thou.
Though it is merely deep, and wide, and shallow as faith.

A Stouffvillite can use the word conservative.
Liberal is spit as a curse.
They will use words never meant for them.
Sharp words that cut, except buttered up and slathered thick with
    elderberry jam.
In truth a Stouffvillite is neither a stove or light.
There can be warmth in their embrace, though they sometimes sear.
Brightness in their smile, though faded, like a bulb about to burn out.

When I go back to Stouffville, I skirt the edge of Markham.
Flitting over their head where the gold topped coronet of a mosque
    is given the silent treatment.
Life goes construction, construction, construction, avert your eyes.

I wave to the Muslims, who we're not getting along with on account
    of their values hitting too close to home.
We had a tug of war with a cute top we both wanted.
It tore down the middle. Now no one can have it.
The shops lining the streets only sell to us now so there is no more fighting.
Then Stouffville goes construction, speed bump, construction, speed
    bump, construction, speed bump, goodbye Muslims.

You never forget how to be from Stouffville when you're from Stouffville.
It's like walking a tight-rope with an ape.
Keswick is a spare town in case Stouffville goes flat,
Or more likely bursts from being filled with too much air.
Though I don't think Stouffville will be going anywhere soon.
The truck has been on cinder blocks in the front yard for years.

I live now in Kitchener, home of vehicles both imported and domestic.
We have a love-hate relationship with the car plant on the edge of town.
The city's meandering streets will lead you in circles.
They were once only corduroy roads, the paths of least resistance,
    formed by horse and buggy trails of a time gone by.
A time that still remains, just north of the city.
Our weeds are taking over, encroaching on our neighbours, creeping.
But so is my dress size.
Suddenly there's so much hollowness to fill with idle thoughts.

In Ontario the Provincial joy is a midwinter night.
"Saint Peter, send us a cold, crisp snowfall, a white dusting to cover
    up all this dirt."
This is how we sound in December on the eve of our Holy Saviour's birth.
There is never enough snow for Stouffville, but Christmas lasts a
    fortnight.
We are a people who want to cast curses on the earth for daring to evolve.
"What sins of our father?" is Stouffville's motto.
There is a day in October when we are all astronauts or knights
    templar, time warpers are everywhere, and Cardinals are asked
    by young ladies to help them soar away.

Red feathers are strewn through the streets, being trampled by the people in their Canadian tuxedos.
When a girl elopes with a cardinal, when she weaves herself a daisy chain crown and dons an orange wedding dress, you know where she's from.

In this way we have raised you up in the way you should go.
Let us all turn green as the fields that hem us in.
Let us all be hard done by.
Grant us minds like a bear trap.
Grant us grade A maple syrup.
Grant us buckets of paint.
And the wisdom to wield the brush.

# THIS MAN
## — *Nicole Schroeder* —
### NON-FICTION

I KNOW this man.

I met him maybe three weeks ago.

He sat on his swivel stool, behind his computer screen, and told me, using his best *I'm a professional and you are not* voice, that I had nothing to worry about. That my son had nothing more than a viral infection. That my son would be running around again in no time.

How wrong he was.

Now, as I sit cradling my listless one-and-a-half year old son, I watch this same man enter the hospital room. I watch his demeanour shift as the other doctor, the doctor whose care my son has been under for almost five days, introduces him to me. I watch him extend his hand before mine. I watch recognition consume his face. I watch as he inhales, and confidently exhales, remarking that he remembers me. He wants me to find the humour within this acknowledgement; even more so, he wants me to find the grace within this moment.

But, I don't find either.

Maybe we wouldn't be here, be in this nauseating hospital room, if he had trusted my maternal instincts three weeks ago. Maybe we wouldn't have watched the excruciating decline of my son's health if he had taken my concerns to heart. And maybe, we wouldn't now be sitting here, discussing my son's upcoming intubation and immediate air evacuation.

I can hear the medical jargon flowing from his mouth. Words I've encountered many times in the past. Words I thought I'd never need to know again. These words are everywhere in this room. They sputter out of his mouth and buoyantly float around. I have to stifle a very real urge to reach out and grab the words—to throw the words to the ground, to shovel them into the garbage. They don't belong here.

I know I'm nodding. I know they don't expect me to speak; but suddenly, there's a new voice filling the room and I don't immediately recognize it as my own—though it is. It's not shaky and vulnerable, like I feel. It's not sleep deprived and anguish filled, like my body.

No, the Voice is calm. The Voice is confident, and the Voice is collected. This Voice, I think to myself, is going to get me through this moment.

I can hear the Voice coolly articulating some of my son's past. That past intubation nearly killed my son once already. But, I don't hear the Voice divulge those painful memories of me holding my son, just as I am now, when he was whisked away during that unspeakable moment. I don't hear the Voice reveal that I witnessed a team of doctors revive and re-intubate my son. No, the Voice keeps those words inside. Maybe this calm, confident, and collected Voice just can't release those words to this man, in this room. And maybe, no one, including myself, wants to hear them.

The Voice stops talking, and I can suddenly feel the tension in the room. I look to the other doctor to find sympathetic and weary eyes. I look to my husband whose bleak smile offers the Voice a thank you. Finally, I look to the man, expecting to see acknowledgement, expecting to see understanding, but instead I find dismissal. The Voice, no matter how calm, how confident, how collected, is no match for medical expertise.

The room becomes engrossed with silence, and all sets of eyes are avoiding one another, until practical conversation resumes its necessary course.

The man's airy and dismissive tone once again fills the room, "Who will accompany your son during the intubation process?"

Medical procedures are not a place for parents. This is especially true for my husband. But, medical procedures are more importantly not a place for children. And definitely, not a place for children without their parents.

I can hear my husband's already heavy heart drop lower in his body. I can feel his gaze against the wall, and I can almost taste the salty tear slowly descending on his cheek. His fatherly ache to protect his son is ravaging his body, but his inability to perform this duty is devastating his mind. We both know that I will be the one accompanying our son.

As I gather my courage and assemble my armour, the Voice speaks again. The Voice tells my husband to leave the hospital. To catch the next flight out. To call my parents. To call his parents.

My husband responds well to the Voice, packs his things, kisses our son's forehead, and dials my parents as he exits the room.

I am left holding my son, absent-mindedly wiping his brow clean of the sweat he had accumulated simply by breathing. I am left waiting to be told what to do next, although I already know exactly what there is left to do.

As the man and the air evacuation team scoop my son from my arms, I silently begin to pray a very simple prayer: *Lord, please help me to have faith, and to trust this man.*

We walk down the small hallway to make our way to the procedure room, and I am greeted with hesitant smiles and inadvertent stares from patients and staff alike. It seems that everyone, regardless of medical background, can sense the additional weight this short walk piles onto my shoulders.

The very first time my son was brought to an intensive care environment, every machine the room housed appeared to be a tool of torture—appeared to be a tool specifically devised to scream of my limited understanding of the medical world, of the world on which my son's survival was dependent. But now, the familiarity of the machines bring me peace and help redirect my focus to my son.

However, my focus is short-lived and broken by the sound of the man's voice. It takes me a second or two to find him in the room, and upon finding him, I am immediately filled with unease, and perhaps even a little disgust. This man, the man that is about to intubate my son, the man that dismissed me three weeks ago, the man that dismissed me five minutes ago—this man is casually leaning against a machine, and in-between stifled yawns, reminds me what I am about to witness will be difficult to watch. I swallow the immediate anger rushing through my veins and instead offer a curt nod, and begin to pray my prayer again.

The procedure begins, and I stiffen my back to stand straighter. I am tall and lean and unmoving, as if I believe that even the most silent of sounds would jeopardize this man's ability to successfully perform intubation on my son.

It doesn't take long, and soon the tube is in place. The man offers me a quick glance, and I am told by a nurse to return to the hospital room.

Upon returning, I barely have enough time to sit on the bed and fold my hands, before an alarm is sounding. The chilling words *code blue* angrily shout through the sound system, penetrating every ounce of the hospital. Nurses are dropping things, sprinting out of rooms, and running down the hallway. I don't need to hear the room number announced to know my son is the cause of the code blue.

An elderly patient peers out from her room and haphazardly declares, "That's the code for someone is dying."

My hands remain clasped and my head remains high.

I sit this way for what feels like eternity, just waiting for someone to come. Surely, someone will come. Someone will save me from this moment. Someone will unclasp my hands and rest my head.

A nurse walks in first. Tears are evident on her cheeks, though they have been wiped away. The two short words out of her mouth almost send me into shock, and while she knowingly repeats them for my benefit, I know it is for her benefit as well: "He's okay. He's okay. He's okay."

Our doctor enters shortly after, slips an arm around my shoulder, and vaguely recounts some of what had just occurred.

Then the man walks into the room. He runs a quick hand through his hair and takes his time finding my eyes.

I patiently wait.

I watch his gaze go from his shoes, to the doctor, and finally to me.

Nobody says a word for the silence speaks louder than any words ever could.

It would be so easy to scream, to vehemently announce my uncontrollable anger. To unleash the recklessness the Voice had so eloquently hid earlier. To finally have my voice heard.

But instead, I find myself acknowledging the humour within this moment. I find myself warmly embracing the grace within this moment.

*This Man.*

The air evacuation team intrudes on our moment and suddenly the world is set back in motion. Our medical journey must continue as my son's quest for wellness is not over.

But...

*This Man* saved my son.

# EULOGY TO THAT FROZEN BANANA
## — *Corals Zheng* —
### SHORT PROSE

How strange, how past memories can sometimes suddenly whelm up, likened to the blur of a red light before the impact—shamefully embodied in the uncanny sight of a brown banana seasoned with sidewalk salt, a single brown curve that dares to stand between you and your destination.

Memory is like this single brown banana, jumping out of nowhere with a malicious, indignant presence, resentful of its untimely passing. *I was supposed to be someone's lunch,* it says, *I wasn't supposed to have gone to waste.* In that sense, you feel pity for the banana, but you walk on, feeling how you would feel when someone doesn't clean up after their dog. You don't think much about the banana until there are four walls around you, until you're alone, until the lock clicks, and only then, the image drips into the black of the iris, drop by drop, until the sink spills over, and I'm crying. You're crying. We're crying for a rotten banana who travelled from Ecuador to become someone's lunch, but it is now frozen in the snow, too hard, too salty to be turned into banana bread.

To christen its memory, I will write a short story of how the banana came to be abandoned:

Our banana was planted two years ago, from a bulb, in Ecuador, a sunny place, a humid place that rains a lot. This banana came from a tree rooted in pitch black soil unearthed from a jungle clearance, where non-bananas migrated to the city to look for work. The banana plant was sprayed with pesticides, and grown in polyethylene bags to prevent spoilage via insects, birds, and generally served as a nice precursor to its supermarket fate. Our banana was picked while it was still green, sorted, and shipped 5,056 km to their marketplace where it is preferred that they are nice and in reasonable bunches. They should be taken to a good home with a wide yard, but this is Toronto so most immigrants begin in small spaces: in this case, a fridge or a pantry unit. The banana faced discrimination and was not picked for a while on account that it was so green, and eventually as it reached its peak, our banana was broken from the bunch, and shoved into a bag to be taken to school. There the banana slipped out of the bag through a hole, and fell on Bloor St, thinking it had finally achieved total freedom, before the snow fell, and it began to regret its decision to come to Canada—but it wasn't really its decision so our banana existed in a state of paradoxical agency and non-agency. Where the gleaming yellow of its skin faded to a nasty brown, a giant bruise surfaced from the stem to the little black bit at the bottom, and the colour grew so uniform that it was almost aesthetically pleasing. Our banana was promised, sold to someone with a purpose—and now it's stuck in limbo, on the street, in a gross state of frozen and rotten, like, nature couldn't even figure out what to do with it. Actually, nevermind nature, she has a different opinion on the state of banana monoculture, so she expressed the distaste with a mass fungal banana extinction. Our banana may very well be the last banana ever.

*The author strongly disapproves of reading the short story as a metaphor for the immigrant experience, or other likewise nonsense.*

# GLASS
## — *Alicia Thiessen* —
### FICTION

I RECOGNIZE his eyes instantly, despite the fact that most of his features are obscured by shadows and by the pulsating blue glow from the overhead bulbs. Through the throngs of bodies writhing together in disjointed unison or shouting at each other over the noise, I know it's him. The light from the bar somewhere in the corner softens his silhouette so that he seems to be some kind of distorted angel.

I leave my friends wordlessly and begin to snake my way through arms and legs, ignoring grinding hips, tongues sampling other mouths. I'm briefly distracted from my mission as I feel crushed glass beneath my feet and regret wearing strappy sandals. My feet are sticky. Drink, probably. Maybe blood. At least it's too dark to see the damage. I wriggle my poor toes, letting some of the loose glass escape, and then continue my awkward gait across the room.

As I pause at a mirrored pillar to set down what's left of my mostly-ice drink, I see no trace of the girl I used to be. How different she was from the blonde before me now, vanished under sharply lined eyes, dark lashes, cherry red lips. I wonder if Matt will even remember me—Matt, who used to shock me in twelfth grade Biology with tales of parties and drunken brawls that both horrified and entranced my innocent imagination.

The last time he saw me, it was a night like this.

Throbbing music. Throbbing bodies.

I was a mess in his hotel room after grad. My first time, but not his.

I suddenly need him to be impressed with my toned calves and grown-up shape—the new version of his wide-eyed conquest.

I'm almost there now, trying to breathe normally, adjusting my low top, straightening my shoulders. I open my mouth to speak, but he's too quick and says my name with that familiar, easy smile I remember like a photograph. "Emma Wilson."

I return his greeting, pretending to be surprised, asking vaguely, "Matt, right?" as if I don't quite remember. We're standing there, two not-quite-strangers, and I know that now is my chance—my only chance—to press my body against his and make him forget the naive girl I was five years ago. I could show him, couldn't I, that there were no hard feelings, despite everything that happened afterwards?

Instead, we chat about nothing—who we've seen lately, how often we come here—all those meaningless details exchanged by old acquaintances. Finally, he reaches out to shake my hand but holds it instead. He leans in close to me; before he can say anything, I whisper into his ear, with finality, "It was nice seeing you again."

He's silent for a moment—surprised, perhaps, that I stopped him—and then says, "You too."

He straightens and I smile at him once, gently pulling my hand away. I'm not sure, but I think I feel his eyes following me as I disappear again into the crowd. I don't like the way it feels anymore. I wish I'd told him instead how I'm only here for a friend's birthday, or how I volunteer with the community centre in my neighbourhood and work two jobs. How I'm halfway through my nursing degree.

What am I even doing here? It's getting late and the twins start kindergarten tomorrow—and I promised them blueberry pancakes in the morning. Besides, the babysitter said she charges double after midnight. I search for a restroom to pull the shards from my feet.

# CYCLE
## *— Erin Alladin —*
### POETRY

Home to the woods!
I dress myself in
Childhood clothes of
Leaf and lichen, zip up
My pine bough cloak, toss on
A scarf of asters, pin
Stars in my hair and shoe
My feet in evening dew.
I trail a cloud of leaf-mold perfume
Back to the city.

Time passes. Moss dries.
    Petals fall.
And here I am on the pavement

Shivering.

# TIME INFINITE SQUARED
## — *Jennie Hunter* —
### FICTION

# 1 MONTH 1 Day
05:11

Giggling, the toddler runs into her bedroom. The child pours coffee beans on her head. A mixture of colours: poppy, marigold, dirt, roses. Like Smarties. How many has it eaten? Will she ever get the baby to sleep again? She wakes up. The baby is gurgling. She pushes off her heavy duvet and the cold air slaps against her skin. The baby grows silent.

5:12

She climbs back into bed; it's still warm. Instantly, the baby cries.

05:14

She feeds the baby in bed and a giraffe walks in the door. It bends its long, puzzled neck and looks down at them with large, coffee brown eyes.

The giraffe whispers something in her ear. What was it? She didn't quite catch it. If only—

05:15

The baby is still in its crib, crying. She gets up, feeds it, and then finds she cannot fall asleep. She goes downstairs to make a cup of coffee. By the time her husband wakes, she's had three large 'World's Best Mom' mug-fulls. The baby has still not woken. She gives her husband a travel mug full of coffee, a kiss on the cheek, and then he's gone.

05:30

She thinks of the job she's on break from. She wonders if there has been any interesting science news, so she Googles it on her iPad and falls asleep after reading: Researchers made an important—

06:25

The baby wakes and fusses for an hour, waves balled fists at invisible ghosts that won't let it sleep. She tries reading the scientific article out loud—after all, it put her to sleep. The baby cries harder. She picks up the iPad, forgets the article, and bounces the child until her arms go numb. She stops bouncing and the baby softly exhales against her shoulder and closes its eyes. She places it gently in the crib so she doesn't wake it. She spends the next hour with her hand on its belly, because the moment she lifts her fingers it screams.

10:01

There's a puddle of drool under her cheek. The baby is two and walking around the house with a bright red travel mug of coffee and a manuscript composed of shopping receipts. It sees her and howls, "I want my teddy!" The coffee mug tips back. She reaches for it, but she isn't quick enough. Hot liquid scalds the toddler's skin. It screams louder. She jolts awake to find that the drool wasn't part of the dream. Thankfully, the coffee was. Her husband is still at work with the offending coffee cup, which saves it from being thrown in the garbage.

10:32

She puts the baby in the swing and lies on the soft, beige carpet. The floor takes the weight off her shoulders and soon she's flying. Her wings are white, fluffy and sparkling like a unicorn's. There's a rainbow in the distance. She squints. Is it made of Skittles? She continues to fly, bobbing through blue skies filled with marshmallow-white clouds. There's a quick trill of unease. She turns, glances around, sees nothing. When she turns back around, the sky is no longer blue. The earth is above her now and it's brown and slick, falling toward her. She kicks out and is surprised to find that she has horse hooves. The world slips away. She is in a dark meadow. There is a scream. She looks down and sees a baby, whimpering. She reaches to pick it up, but she no longer has hands.

10:36

She jerks awake. The baby whimpers and pinches its eyes shut. She watches it for two minutes. Three. It sleeps soundly. She shakes her head and lays down.

11:00

The sound isn't quite right. It's too exact. Short, tonal bursts. Wavering, varying in volume and in length. She steps up to the blackboard and begins to write an equation. She draws a sinusoidal curve. She marks down moments of sound. One at a time, ticking the chalk along the line. This will be a breakthrough. She will win the Nobel Prize for this work. But the noise keeps coming, distracting her from the math. She tries to ignore it, but she can't. The board goes fuzzy. Bright light pushes into her eyelids.

11:01

There it is again. It starts. Comes again. Then a pause. Then again. What is that? Is it the baby? Maybe she should lift her head, just peek with one eye. The baby is still sleeping. Whatever is bothering her isn't bothering it. Oh. Wait. The noise comes again. It's the phone. It's him. Are you okay? You didn't answer.

I was sleeping.

Oh. Right.

11:03

She goes downstairs to make another cup of coffee. The internet says she should sleep when the baby sleeps but he just reminded her that they're having company for dinner. They agreed to order food, but still, the house is a mess. She'll just clean up a little bit. She's too on edge to sleep now anyway. Just a few dishes, load and unload the dishwasher, a few pots. Coffee will perk her up. Maybe just a couple Cheetos as a treat. She'll sleep when the baby sleeps next time.

12:12

She leans over the swing and stares down at the baby. It's still sleeping. It never sleeps this long. Now she's had so much coffee she doesn't think she'll ever sleep. But she lies down anyway, because, well, the baby is sleeping.

12:19

She's in a train station that's supposed to be in Montreal but it looks more like Vancouver and there, to the east, are the mountains, which climb up and up and up and up. She's going to take the train to the mountains, because the sensei who appears in red robes tells her this is her task. First, she must pick the right train. No trains arrive. She waits and waits but there are no trains. She leaps down onto the tracks and begins walking toward the mountains, but somehow, she ends up on a flat, beige expanse of beach running off into deep blue ocean. The city has disappeared. Then, out of the water, a crying baby, floating toward her on a green leaf, a wall of water heading straight for it. She panics, dives in.

12:22

She wakes up and the baby is awake too. Crying loudly because the blanket has fallen off and it must be cold, not to mention hungry because it has been forever since it fed. She uncovers herself and pulls the baby onto her, feeling the awkward tug and sharp pain of the latch, which she has to correct before her nipples bleed again. She shoves her finger in, shifting things around until it feels right, until she feels nothing but the soft, warm, tiny body against hers.

12:55

Time has passed. The change is displayed brightly by the small clock on the bookshelf across the room but she doesn't know where the minutes have gone. The baby is almost done and she feels energetic, so she dresses the baby up to take it for a walk.

13:13

Outside it is cool and the trees are yellow with autumn. She doesn't know what happened to summer. She recalls that there was a big deadline at her job, and that someone else is dealing with that now. She thinks about calling in to check, then realizes she's left her cell phone back at the house and knows that her husband is trying to call her just then. She worries he'll panic if he can't get a hold of her so she turns back. Two blocks from the house she runs into Vicky, who also has a baby. They went to high school together and used to be vaguely friendly but never friends. Now, Vicky wants to have playdates. She looks at her baby; it doesn't play yet. Maybe her baby appears advanced. Vicky's baby is a round, fat six-month-old that she thought was closer to a year. Vicky's baby has a hand shoved in its mouth all the way up to the third knuckle. Saliva drips down its arm. Her own baby is beginning to look sleepy again. It rolls onto its side and begins to fuss. She passes her number over to Vicki and then tells Vicki she has to go home; she's expecting a call.

13:51

There are no messages. To comfort herself, she turns the television to General Hospital and makes a mug of hot chocolate before the baby demands to be fed. It falls asleep on her breast, and barely stirs as she moves it to the bassinet. She stretches across the leather couch, which is cool on her cheek. She tries to keep her eyes open, but she falls into a deep, deep slumber.

19:00

The dinner party is grand, with sequinned dresses and black, enamelled plates that sparkle under the gigantic chandelier her husband had installed that afternoon. A French nanny walks in and takes the baby away. She doesn't know the nanny, but she doesn't worry. The nanny has everything under control. The wine was imported directly from the Côtes Du Rhône, where she'll be heading next week for a mathematics conference. She's up for an award for proving that mathematics is all that's needed to properly raise a fussy child. She slips into a puffy pink gown for the ball. The orchestra arrives and sets up in the ball room, which is attached to the living room. She twirls away into the night. Has a fabulous time in France, and returns just in time for the baby's graduation.

**1 Month 2 Days**

09:12

Her friends text message that they had a wonderful time the previous night, but feel bad that she had to do so much, because she seemed tired. They felt really bad when she dropped the takeout container of Ginger Beef all over the breast pump. If she ever wants a break, she should let them know. How about now? After all, she only got about two hours of sleep all night. Well, they are both at work because they still have jobs at the edge of science and submissions to technical journals have to be completed. But otherwise they totally would. Maybe on the weekend. Or next Tuesday night. That might work. She knows she will forget this offer. She has a feeling they know she will forget too.

**1 Month 3 Days**

01:01

The baby did not sleep all day. Finally it is resting. Or dead. She stares at it, checking that it is breathing before she finally lays down herself and closes her eyes. Her boss is angry that she hasn't finished the report. She looks over at her subject and types: PROOF, she then follows this up with a list of things: sucks on the second knuckle of the pointer finger; occasionally sucks at the inside of wrist before scrunching up face and switching to finger; takes deep breath every two minutes; eyes do not fully close but remain open—here she stops, stands up, and takes her ruler to the baby. She measures the distance between the top eyelid and the bottom. She returns to her desk to continue the report. Her boss yells at her. She types: 2mm. Then she looks up at the bright, round light above her head and types: time infinite circle dividing space by people takes away space resulting in negative time. She swivels in her chair and hands the report to her boss. It is printed on paper bright as fresh blood. He takes the pages and eats them up.

**1 Month 4 Days**

01:03

The baby again did not sleep all day but two nights in a row the baby has now fallen asleep at the same time. Surely this is a good thing. The establishment of pattern. Pattern, routine, expected behaviour. This is what she needs.

03:14

She feeds the baby. Her head lulls to her breast. She jerks awake, thinking she has dropped the baby, but it's still in her arms.

06:18

She feeds the baby. Or she dreams she feeds the baby. Or she has been feeding the baby all night. She isn't sure which one is the truth.

10:30

She takes the baby on a mall walk. She read that it may need stimulation in order to determine what regular hours are. She thinks of all the nights she went out late when she was pregnant, thinks the creation of this night owl is all her fault. If only she had gone to bed at eight o'clock every night in her third trimester she could have taught the child in utero that night is the time to be quiet, be still, and not be hungry. Instead, she stayed up late, attempting to compress the world into a small ball of numbers.

12:00

The child likes the mall. It likes the light filtering through the atrium and the sound of children laughing at the small indoor playground. She eats some french fries, then later, a cheeseburger. She looks at the shops, at the dresses she hopes to fit in a couple of months, at the high heeled shoes she vows she will never wear again. She grabs a coffee at Starbucks and straps the kid into the car.

13:00

The baby has fallen asleep in its carseat and she fears to wake it. She parks in the attached garage and closes the door, turns the vehicle off, and lays back in her seat to take a nap.

16:07

She wakes with a sharp kink in her neck. The baby is cooing in the backseat. They get out of the car and go into the house. She lays the baby down on a playmat in a bright spot of sunlight. It glows and tries to bat at the giggling worms dangling above its head. She puts the frozen lasagna brought over by the neighbour in the oven and reads a couple blogs on parenting while she waits for her husband to come home.

22:34

Her husband has gone to bed but the baby is still awake so she rocks it in the nursery and sings it silly songs: The Ants Go Marching, Ten Little Monkeys, The Itsy-Bitsy Spider. The baby falls asleep on schedule and she climbs into her bed with her husband, who is snoring loudly. She's so tired that the rattle and stop of the train pulling into the station doesn't keep her awake.

**1 Month 5 Days**

07:00

She wakes up and leaps over to the bassinet. The sun shining through her curtains is all wrong. The baby has not woken all night, surely it is dead. It is there, breathing. It opens its eyes. They are blue. He smiles, reaches out. Phoebe reaches in.

# WILL'S JACKPOT
## — *John Alpaugh* —
### NON-FICTION

ON NORTHERN Nova Scotia's Cape Breton Island, the Cabot Trail winds through ancient rolling highlands and floats across sea cliffs above the Atlantic Ocean. Before this summer, I had toured the Trail only once, for two days last fall with my good friends, Geoff Richards and Jack Irvine, and Jack's Irish setter, Hazel. Stopping at various lookouts, trailheads, and beaches, we saw firsthand why it is a world-famous piece of road. On the 298km, two-lane loop, I fostered a love for the land it travelled through and vowed to return, next time as a resident.

Such is the case as we drive north of Ingonish onto the smooth roads of Cape Breton Highlands National Park, repaved in anticipation of Canada 150 celebrations. We are making our way to Black Brook Beach, a known surf break that is rumoured to work with a Northeastern Swell, such as the one we enjoy today. On a day in late May, it is sunny and 17C, the warmest we have had to date.  The hills are showing their first hints of summer green and the deep aqua water below us is glistening. I sit in the passenger seat of an early 2000s Subaru Forester my friend, Will MacLachlan, has recently purchased from an elderly couple in Halifax, where we live as students for eight months of the year with Geoff and Jack. He sits behind the wheel. Other than the fading signage of the car's name on its rear door, of which only the first 'e' remains, the car is in perfect shape, thanks to years of dutiful care. Its Nova Scotia license plate reads "Canada's Ocean Playground" and the spacious rear of the active station wagon holds our surfboards, thick wetsuits, and some camera gear.

Will looks out over the glistening deep blue hood in front of us through brown Ray-Ban's, his curly blonde hair falling out the hole of his backwards snapback. A smile spreads across his face. He can barely contain his excitement for a day we have spent a month waiting for. Will had never been to Cape Breton before deciding to call it home for the summer—he was not able to join us on our road trip last fall—but our stories were enough for him to follow us up in search of days like today. With the windows rolled down, the air in the car is electric.

At each lookout, a new glimpse of the shore is presented to us, and each raises our hopes for the break at Black Brook. Will's excitement is spilling out as we draw closer to our realized dream born in the fall. Surfing in Cape Breton. Today is the first day we have had even a moderately hopeful surf report, and we are eager to test its accuracy, if we are not already overconfident. Each corner we pass overlooking the shore is more promising than the last, shapely waves breaking close. Looks can be deceiving in this part of the province however. Weather is subject to stark, drastic changes that leave plans unfulfilled. There is no choice but to take what is given and make the best of it.

We make the last turn on the Cabot Trail ahead of Black Brook Beach, and a view of the break opens up. Will pulls into the lookout above the beach. The surf is calm. The swell direction is slightly off plane with the shore-break of the beach and is blocked by surrounding points. It has missed. The air inside the Forester is suddenly as flat as the break, and the smile rushes away from Will's face. Our enthusiasm has evaporated, we have sobered up, and for a moment we pause. What now?

Below one of the promising lookouts we passed further south on the Cabot Trail, about halfway between Black Brook Beach and Ingonish, is a spot we came across on our short journey in the fall. Jack Irvine had provided the transportation, and being a surfer himself, he had all of his surf gear along in the truck with him. We were heading south, nearing Ingonish and the end of our tour, when we came across this spot which looked to be supplying a break. It was below an 80 foot cliff of sand and rock, but Jack fearlessly slid down in his wetsuit, using his board to balance, while Geoff and I watched with Hazel from above, taking photos. The water was clear and glassy, but the waves were slow and small. Jack managed to catch a few before he somehow scaled the cliff and returned to his truck parked on the side of the Trail. It was not the best surfing he had ever done, but it showed promise for days with more swell, especially when, around the next bend, we passed a shallow brook leading to the beach, saving us any more risky trips up and down the steep cliffs.

This comes to mind as Will and I sit in disappointment, and before long we are back on the road headed to Jack's spot. From the lookout, it seems to be working. We reach the brook we missed in the fall, and are soon suited up and wading in the ankle-deep water flowing towards the mouth in the beach. Our excitement is back, this time a bit more subdued, weary of the failure we may have to endure.

When we get to the break at the far end of the beach, below the cliffs, it appears quite rocky under the rough grey-blue water. Living in Halifax for school, Will has had the opportunity to learn to surf at the many breaks near the city, like Lawrencetown and Cow Bay. I have not had as much time in the water—I have never stood up on a wave—and in this unfamiliar break I am not completely comfortable, so I begrudgingly decide to stay ashore for the time being. But Will is experienced and eager, and he charges in. This is the moment he has been waiting for. And it's here for the taking.

The break is sporadic. Will drifts around for a while trying to find the ideal spot for today's swell, finally settling about 50m from the shore. The first set is coming in, and Will paddles into the second wave. He pops up quickly to his feet, the wave propels him towards shore. It crashes down behind him and out of the white froth his arms shoot up in celebration. A moment of pure ecstasy. I can see his wide, white smile from my spot on the rocky beach.

After an hour in the water, Will has caught a few waves before taking one back to shore. He says this is why he came to Cape Breton, for these experiences. His sea charged vitality is contagious. After sitting on the beach in my own disappointment, I feel compelled to give it a shot in a smaller, seemingly safer part of the break. His simple joy has removed any pressure from the act of surfing, and it is pure play in Canada's Ocean Playground. At first we flop around, body surfing in the shore break, but we quickly grab our toys. We paddle out a little way and below us is only rocks. We are too focused on the waves to care. I'm floating on my board, and after a few pointers, Will encourages me to paddle into a wave. I catch it and glide towards the shore on my stomach. I'm at the hump in my development as a surfer he says, the point where I can control myself in the water but I cannot yet ride a wave. He says the next step is learning which waves to try to catch, and he assures me I'll be standing on a wave soon. I am not so sure, but it's difficult to be too upset with my ineptitude considering my present position: in the long shadows of the high sea cliffs of Cape Breton, on a private beach with one of my best friends, whose spirits could not be higher.

Today was the dream we had on the road last fall, and as we pull back onto the Cabot Trail heading home, we are already dreaming of the next day like it.

# WITHOUT HER
## — *Heather McLeod* —
### FICTION

EVEN I could see that the dog had more than a few extra pounds to lose, but who was I to give him that sort of unsolicited advice? Too many years of living with my mother had made me immune to even the most subtle suggestions of self-betterment and I had long since promised myself that I would not grow up to be like her.

She would have freaked out if she saw us sitting here; the damp earth soaking slowly up through the denim fabric of my jeans. Her freak out would be silent, a kind of inner battle that would move slowly across her face, starting at her lips and ending up in her forehead where it would writhe a while before finally disappearing into her hairline. No words accompanied this dance—and to be honest, they weren't needed.

Her body had this way of spelling out exactly what she was thinking. The way her eyes threatened to bug out of her head when you helped yourself to seconds or the way her tongue balled up in her mouth until she was practically choking when you came down the stairs wearing clothing that fit a little too tightly or a skirt that hung an inch too short. The pressure would build up inside her until with a bang the kitchen would receive a complete overhaul—needed or not—and the clatter of pots and pans would fill the silence while the roar of the vacuum cleaner sucked up any of the unsaid words that stubbornly clung to us.

I was twelve when I discovered a perverse kind of pleasure in making her freak out.

Little things at first, like wearing lipstick or rolling up the waistband of my skirt and then bigger things; dying my hair red, wearing black *all* the time, getting my lip pierced. In a way it was like catching a wasp in a cup; a sudden head rush of power from holding such a desperately angry creature hostage.

It took me a while to get my life together enough that I could move out. After finishing college, I found myself still living at home trying to scrape together enough cash to make both first and last month's rent and when I finally did, I still needed her name on the rental agreement. Like no one believed I could make it on my own. She signed the paper with a sigh that said I wasn't anything without her to which I responded by ripping it out of her hands and stalking off. I was everything without her.

As soon as I got the apartment, I packed up my stuff and left. She stood in the doorway watching me, a small frown on her face. She called me every day, twice a day, for the next two weeks. Most of the time I didn't answer. Then I bought her the dog. Out loud I said it was a thoughtful gift—something to occupy her time now that I wasn't there. But, inside I knew it was a parting shot—another chance to see her face dance.

Except it totally backfired.

She loved the dog. You could just tell by the way her rules got all crumpled up. She barely called me anymore—once a week if that—and then only to talk about him. I thought about letting the rent slide, about getting kicked out and moving back in with her. But I didn't—it just wouldn't be the same now that she had him.

The dog was the only one with her when she died from the heart attack. Or at least, that's what the neighbour told me. Said she kept hearing a strange noise, like a siren, coming from inside the house. The dog was lying beside the body, howling. I've heard that animals can tell when death is coming, like maybe they can smell it or something. I've always had a sensitive nose but it's hard to smell something when you are miles away.

Standing in the house without her, I freaked out. It was like somehow she had gotten mixed up inside me—I felt my face twitching, my eyes bulging. I couldn't believe she had gone and died on me. There was no one but the dog to watch as I banged the clean kitchen pots around, scrubbing them furiously in the silence. Only the dog heard the roar of the vacuum as it spluttered and choked on the empty air. When I shut it off, he was sitting at the door whining.

I let him out and followed him as he snuffled across the sidewalk, sniffing at something I couldn't see. Part of me wondered if he was looking for her. And even though I knew it was probably nothing more than a trail of old dog pee, I let him go where he wanted. He headed down the old dirt trail to the lake, the one I always took when I was mad at her. I used to throw my rusty bike down in the dirt, whip stones into the water, and think about how much I hated her.

The lake is covered in tiny ripples as the water winks and shimmers in the late afternoon light. The dog sits with his tongue out, his ribs heaving. I sit next to him, my shoulders slumped in automatic defeat. I lean my head over into the pillow of fat around his neck and close my eyes—who am I without her? I sigh and the dog whines—a thin little sound that gets carried away on the wind. Maybe she was right all along; maybe I could stand to lose a little weight. But all I know right now is that I'm going to keep carrying it around a little while longer, at least until I'm ready to say goodbye.

# COMPASSION
## — *Candace Janelle Ormond* —
### NON-FICTION

NAVIGATING OUR relationships when they change is hard. Trying to selflessly promote and protect others' relationships when yours have changed can be almost punishing.

Everyone says it takes courage to face adversity in our personal lives but they leave out the most important part of that truism. We do need to courageously face our adversities, but if we have the wrong side-kick, we'll find ourselves ill-equipped and suffering. Every interaction will have the explosive potential to become a confrontation if we are operating with courage and angst, or courage and confusion, or courage and shame. All those feelings have the ability to be stronger than our courage if we allow them to thrive, and every negative interaction will feed those emotions.

There is one combination that has been life-changing for me in my journey of healing from the various experiences of loss, betrayal, and grief that I have had in the last couple years. Courage and compassion together have the ability to push us through the most difficult of circumstances with grace and self-respect.

I grieved hard for a long time before my children's father and I separated. I grieved so hard because I was so devastated over how our separating would potentially impact the kids. I thought my one job as a kinkeeper was to protect *them*.

The right job was actually to protect my kids' relationships. I struggled with how to do that. I definitely tried to do it with courage and angst at first and I oftentimes found myself feeling more defeated than empowered. At that point—around one year ago—I was discovering how to have compassion for myself. I wanted to stand up for them and the hurt I knew they were caused by our separation. I wanted to advocate for the relationship I believed they deserved with their father, and I was carrying their pain anytime it didn't add up to the standard I was measuring it by.

I had all levels of support. I had my family, my close friends, and my kids' family—my extended family—while their father, it seemed, had almost no support. He was burdened by everyone's disappointment and expectations and his own shame. As I could feel healing beginning, I started struggling with the dichotomy of my very human heart-driven desire to be empathetic with him while also trying to hold onto injustice because I did not want him to think I accepted him.

That all led to me feeling really conflicted because I wasn't being true to myself. I was trying to manifest self-compassion while also being defensive towards him (in the very minimal times when I would even interact with him). I was filling up with those conflicting energies; and then one day, as I was driving down Franklin Avenue carrying some heaviness on my chest, I passed by a local church. The church has a message board outside where they post a different quote, pun, or beautiful message every week. That particular week when I was searching for answers on how to move forward with my dignity intact without dismissing my own boundaries, the sign read: You Will Never Regret Being Kind.

Wow. As soon as I got a piece of paper and a pen in my hand, I wrote that down and I stuck it in a place where I would be forced to read it every. single. day.

I had to acknowledge that I couldn't be compassionate with myself the way I needed to be if I wasn't willing to be compassionate with someone I had little esteem for at the time. I always regretted being sharp after I spoke to him with self-righteousness, so I knew the sign was right. Because I wouldn't be able to completely respect myself if I was making exceptions in who I was compassionate with. It didn't mean I needed to be fake or pretend to be nice. It meant I needed to **dig deep** to find genuine compassion for another human being despite my own feelings about their actions or any harm I felt they caused me or my kids at any given time. So I started practicing that and it has been a continuous practice. It is also the most imperative thing that allowed me to begin *truly* **healing.**

I started asking deeper questions: How do we navigate being a kinkeeper in the midst of changing dynamics and *why* is it important to do it?

If I had chosen to continue self-protection over self-respect, or if I had kept up the search for reparation over the desire to heal, I would have needed to abandon self-compassion and that was something I was not willing to give up once I discovered the power in it. And if I didn't start acting with compassion towards my children's father I would have been costing them everything that was good in them. Watching us continue to interact in an unhealthy way would have eventually destroyed them, in a more certain way than their parents' separating ever could.

If I disrespected or disregarded a man they love, who is a part of them, I would be, in essence, disrespecting that part of them, too. I would have been damaging their own self-respect, their respect of others, their empathy, their resiliency, their innate kindness, their sense of security and belonging, their ability to accept change, and so much more. *The soul stuff.*

How do we do it? Step by step, day by day, one deep breath at a time. Sometimes it makes the experience of co-parenting and kinkeeping lighter, and sometimes it makes it difficult in a necessary way. If it didn't challenge us, we wouldn't be able to handle the next adversity. There would be nothing to celebrate or achieve.

Maybe our main goal as kinkeepers needs to be more than just promoting and protecting relationships. Somewhere along the way we also need to teach people to do that for themselves, and perhaps the best way to do that is to model compassion.

# SURFACE TENSION
## *— Tracy Evans —*
### POETRY

à propos of nothing, a meditation on stories
because, she says, "Stories stalk us"
And I laughed, imagining the pink purple sunrise that stalks me
    every morning and clubs me over the head
    with beauty and glittering truths about the universe;
Wolves in dark woods;
and dark lumps of bison,
mistaken for rocks on the prairie.
Not the hot-breathed monster
huffing down my neck, reminding me of the fear eaters,
impatient Attention Seekers, shake the bed.
Uninvited stories:
Memories rise from interrupted sleep:
wide-eyed and drowning, just below the surface, kicking, stroking,
    never breaking the surface's tension,
spell cast
surface tension over a moment
unbroken
small, wet shoulders wracked by sobbing. Fished out, choking and
    sputtering, life saved,
admonished for not trying harder.
Stalked by restless stories.
Chapters end.
Years pass.
Newsprint stories
(who even reads on newsprint anymore but doesn't it add to the
    quaintness of this story, stalking?)
Of flashing lights and Tasers
And "nobody knows what happened"

A sad series of unfortunate events:
a Count Olaf, glinting knife, chasing children out the front door.
I wonder still if I had been braver then, if he might still be alive.
Stalked by stories;
but not by gentle giants or fragile laughter.
Desperate monsters
hold sway,
seeking affection.

# ABSENT FRIENDS AND NEW ACQUAINTANCES
## — *David Perlmutter* —
### FICTION

IT WAS pretty simple how we met, really. We were both at the same costume party, and we hooked up based on our common interests.

Well, there *was* a little more to it than that, yes.

I spotted her over by the punchbowl. You couldn't not see her—at least I couldn't. Tall, with bright red hair, red sweater, white skirt, and white shoes. The spitting image of who she was trying to be from TV. From a show long since gone, but well-remembered by those who saw it.

Myself, I hoped that my similarly-designed outfit, based on another similar character from another show of that type, was accurate enough for her to know a) who I was supposed to be and b) that I was tolerable enough to be thought of as a romantic figure, as my TV role model hoped to be thought of vis-à-vis his particular crush. Thus far that night, strikeouts at both ends.

So I gathered myself up, cleared my throat, and spoke to her.

"Shouldn't you be out busting your brothers?" I asked.

Fortunately, she smiled pretty wide, as if to say to me: *You know who I am!* And then she answered:

"I should be asking you the same thing about stopping all that weird supernatural crap that happens on your show. Or maybe just keeping your goofy twin sister in line, huh?"

I gave her back the same smile she gave me, with the same meaning.

Then we hesitated as to what to say next. We clearly had something in common. Neither of us had that glassy-eyed look you get from when you take Computron pills and can project the Internet right in front of your face for hours and hours, just using your hands the way you used to use a mouse in the old days, without the need of any external device to help you get online. We two were both outsiders who refuse to play by the rules of our time by following "trends" and doing what was expected of us, just like those whom we impersonated did. But was it enough for us to connect beyond that?

Fortunately, she broke the silence first.

"It must've really been hell coming down here in this weather just dressed in that getup," she said. "My damn legs are still freezing from walking down here. Stupid winter!"

"Yeah," I responded. "This is what happens when two fictional characters made for summer end up stuck in the middle of winter. But you took a bigger risk, since you got longer legs to freeze."

"I suppose," she answered. "Anybody here know who you were— or, I should say, *are*?"

"Not a clue," I said. "They figured me for some kind of midget adventurer type."

"Well, that's who he was. 'Cept he wasn't a midget."

"Unlike me. It's not fun being a short guy when you have to look up to everybody."

"Better than hitting your head on crap all the time, and having to get things down from the shelf 'cause you're the only one who can reach them."

"There are bad things to everything."

"You know something? I think the two of them could have made a good couple if there'd ever been a cross-over between the shows."

"You think?"

"Sure. He was real good at finding out the truth about stuff—even if he didn't want to. She wanted to find a sure-fire way of making sure her mom saw what her brothers were doing, in an honest, no B.S. way. Sounds like a good match."

"Too bad it didn't happen."

"Not in *their* worlds." Suddenly, she had extended her hand for me to grasp, as if she were an Elizabethan lady extending a dance invite to a gentleman of that time. "But that doesn't mean it can't happen in *ours*."

And so, we got together and danced. And we decided to stay together after, from then right up until now.

And nobody had better tell us TV cartoons from way back in the 21st century, viewed and reviewed on ancient DVDs, aren't good for anything. Because we know better.

# THE BAR ON THE HILL
## — *Kim Losier* —
### NON-FICTION

I GLANCE around the tired room with the worn varnished hardwood floors and the pollution-coated hazy panes of glass, and I sense the weight of countless life stories contained within these dingy walls. The haggard and weary looking arrivals sit comfortably around the dark oak pub tables. The deep lines etched in bloated faces scream of broken dreams and years of hard living in this industrial blue collar town situated on the rugged shores of the Bay of Fundy.

There are exceptions, of course, like the cute twenty-something raven haired indie singer with black lipstick, torn leggings, and soft leather flats. She sits at the bar with her boyfriend, sipping a cold Moose Light, flinging one leg back and forth, patiently waiting for her turn at the microphone.

A steaming hot Keith Urban look-alike—skinny jeans and cropped mousy blonde hair—leans against the pale green paint-chipped wall, his hand resting on a sticker-laden guitar case. The white haired businessman with the long black Burberry coat looks familiar. He grins like he's won the lottery as he drapes his arm around the attractive, smartly dressed woman with long auburn hair and perfect makeup.

A tarnished brass ship's bell tinkles as the weathered grey entrance door opens and scrapes across the warped floor. The bass player, wearing a short sleeved tee and Blue Jays ball cap, takes a break and exits the building for a quick puff. I immediately think of the Golden Lion, a popular bar on the east end of town I used to frequent thirty years ago, and I smell the thick smoke-saturated air and cigarettes smouldering in amber glass ashtrays, overflowing with butts and crimped metal beer caps.

Times have changed. Today, the clear smoke-free air reeks of musty brick and stale ale. But as the music and people fill this close space, I find myself drifting back to a time when faces were smooth and life was young and hopeful. A raspy voice belts out a solid version of an old Tom Cochran hit and the music vibrates and pounds loudly in my head. *"Life is a highway, I want to ride it, all night long."*

My life is that highway and my journey on it is winding down. My life mirrors the contents found in the shabby leather wallet tucked inside the pocket of my khaki jacket, depleted and being spent far too quickly. But I find myself enjoying this spring afternoon and ponder why it has taken me more than two decades to revisit what has always made me most satisfied and content: the melding sound of a really tight band, the crashing of brass cymbals, the smooth clean tones of the rhythm guitar, a room permeated with muffled chatter and a sea of moving bodies.

I breathe deeply, inhaling every rhythm and riff, my head nodding as my body consumes every beat. With each note, I feel the vine of anxiety and worry rooted within me weaken as the winding tendrils slowly unravel and release their grip.

I stare at the ink-covered arms of the seasoned drummer wearing a navy blue wool toque and am reminded of the tattoo I promised myself on the birth date of my sixtieth year, but somehow didn't have the nerve. I wasn't strong enough to battle the backlash, the critics; but today, with this rising rebirth, perhaps I might.

The tattoo, a quote I once read by an unknown author, is simple yet profound: *"Music is what feelings sound like."* These six words resonate deep within me. I picture the dark ink letters meandering on the delicate skin just above my wrist, encased with treble clefs, musical notes, and tiny crimson hearts. Right now, at this moment, in this place, where the worn and weary come alive in song, truer words were never spoken.

I close my eyes and embrace the barrage of memories and unlocked emotions and I feel, for the first time in years, invigorated. I sense the beginning of a new season, one of shedding years of self suppression, codependency, and grief.

I note the quick glance from the grey haired man at the next table as he scans the room. Our eyes meet and lock, ever so briefly. I smile. He smiles back. I feel a weak spark struggling to ignite. A dim flicker, a glimmer. And, like those unknown faces around me, I feel the weight of my own life, a complex story woven with incredible joy, sadness, hope, and unfathomable pain. An incomplete writing with blank pages yet to be scripted before the final chapter closes.

The afternoon has slipped by far too quickly. It's getting dark. The bright streetlamp streams a soft glow into the dimly lit room and illuminates the flapping Irish flag that flies outside just above the window casing of the old Victorian building.

The open mic session at the bar on the hill is ending, and as the instruments are laid to rest the crowd rises to their feet, whistling, and clapping their appreciation in deafening unison. Music, the unwavering power that can command our body, heal our soul, and unite total strangers. Yes, indeed, this old town has a ton of talent. Always has, always will.

This was a good day. Long overdue. I raise my glass of Pinot Grigio and propose a toast. "To next Saturday, my friends, I have come home."

# SUMMER
## — *Hina Rani* —
### FICTION

MAYA'S BABY pink nails drummed against the patio table as if to usher in the story that was brewing up above in the late-summer clouds. I examined my own nails: a matching shade of pink, but I had already chipped off most of the paint. I slipped back in my wicker chair, lulled by the sound of her tapping. She stopped abruptly, interrupting my reverie.

"Oh! I almost forgot! I need to show you something."

She reached into her back pocket and pulled out a deck of tarot cards, spreading them face up on the table in front of us. They were creased and rolling up at the edges like pages of a well-loved book. The pencil and watercolour sketches detailed a variety of biblical-looking scenes in muted colours.

"Where did you get these?" I asked, turning over the *Queen of Pentacles* in my hands

"You know that spiritual shop on Main Street? The one with all the dreamcatchers hanging in the windows?"

I thought of the shop with the purple lettered sign that read "Moonflower." It seemed out of place and almost otherworldly compared to the smoothie shop right beside it. Just the kind of place that would interest Maya.

"I'm surprised that place is still running. I've never seen anyone go inside."

She adjusted the strap of her tank top and grinned. I held my breath for a moment, watching the lines that formed by her mouth when she smiled like that. "That's probably why they're going out of business," she said. "I practically got these for free."

I laughed at her inappropriately cheery tone. "You don't even know how to read tarot cards."

"Of course I can." She gathered the cards back into their deck formation and held them out to me. "Choose one."

I picked out a card. *The Hanged Man*. A young man with golden hair hung upside down from a tree. A vine encircled his right ankle and bound it to a branch. The expression on his face was calm and vaguely content, like he did not intend to come down from the tree any time soon. I handed it over to Maya. She examined it.

As she pondered, I fidgeted with the rose charm on my bracelet. Maya had made it for me on my 11th birthday. Sculpting tiny clay charms was one of the many hobbies she'd picked up in all the years I'd known her. I could hardly keep up with all the things she liked to do, but I liked hearing her tell me about them as we sipped pink lemonade on my patio on summer afternoons much like this.

She spoke up. "The hanged man can symbolize a feeling of being stuck. You're unable to move on to something. Like, you know you have to do something, or say something, but you just can't."

I shrugged. "Doesn't mean anything to me."

"No, you're supposed to pick another one, too."

"Now you're just making things up."

"No, I'm serious," she said, holding out the deck once again. I picked out another card.

Two people, presumably Adam and Eve, stood nude in a bush. Large red roses bloomed at their feet. From above, an angel with hair like fire watched them. *The Lovers*. Maya put both cards side by side on the table in front of her. As she studied them, her hair fell in her eyes. Her silence was longer this time. I looked up and quietly watched the clouds get darker.

"So you're stuck, frustrated, and in love," she finally said.

She looked at me but I couldn't look back.

"Something like that." I clenched my jaw to hold back the tears.

Realization flashed in her eyes just as the first raindrop of the end of summer fell from the sky. It landed on *The Lovers* and the red water-coloured roses bled a baby pink.

# TOKYO TOMATO
## —*Jonathan Mendelsohn*—
### NON-FICTION

THEY SAY the hardest truth of travelling is realizing you have to take yourself wherever you go. I'm not so sure. I've been other people all over, like in high school when I pretended I didn't like reading and wore a trench coat downtown so I could smoke cigarettes and perfect my pool game while mimicking Christian Slater's James Dean impression. The good sheep from the suburbs turned baaad, scamming free meals I'd convince fast food managers give me for some "mistake" their employees made the day before (an alleged allergy to onions, say). I'd learn to talk my way into movies, concerts; I even worked my way into a Leafs playoff game once.

I could be other people in Tokyo as well.

I was twenty-five and stuck in the rut of a routine that was killing me. I hadn't gone to Osaka to wear a tie, let alone teach English conversation classes in a dinky little Plexiglass booth all day. Nobody does. Being paid to chat with between one and three Japanese adults may sound great, but soon enough you'd meet every one and exhaust all chatter-worthy material with Hiroki, the retired salaryman who came thrice a week and considered drinking and sleeping his only hobbies. Six months asking Hiroki if he'd done *anything* over the weekend and the Golden Week vacation in May finally arrived. I lost the tie and hopped a bullet train to Tokyo.

In the early 00s, Roppongi Hills was a brand new, ultra-fashionable district of the city. The avant-garde museum that I didn't visit looked cool. I, however, had more pressing matters, namely to catch a glossy Hollywood flick on a big-ass curved screen at the just-opened Toho multiplex. I'd done the major tourist stuff. What I needed were touches of home, or at least the American franchise equivalent, and I'd already had my fill of 100yen McDonald's cheeseburgers. And then some.

After purchasing my ticket for a George Clooney political thriller, I came upon the Tokyo Grand Hyatt (like a regular Hyatt, only a five-star hell of a lot more grand). As I stepped into that modern, minimalist lobby I was walking taller, prouder, imagining myself as *someone*. Not like being rich was a priority. I was an English teacher trying to be a writer. But one classy hotel and suddenly all I ever wanted was a little ritziness in my life. To that point, Japan had been all *ramen* noodles and supermarket sushi. No more. From now on I would be your fancy-pants writer, drinking highballs and banging out stories. Not just writing them, selling them; not just selling, but earning diamonds from 'em. Oh yeah, a regular F. Scott Fitzgerald. I liked that. F. Scott. Just like that. I wasn't all suited up, but so what. I had my journal. A couple pens. They were in my knapsack and I was wearing hiking shoes, but not to worry. So long as I felt it. They'd see. They'd know. Just think it: F. Scott, F. Scott.

The image of the scotch on the rocks at the classy hotel bar—it's always been a favourite. The ice tinkling against the glass as I down my drink. The fantasy suitably rounded out when the lady smoking beside me asks me back to her room. The illusion shattering realities of budget and knapsack the only hindrances to the plot. Never mind. The idea was to get a free drink or two. I'd go in for the old 'journalist doing a story' bit. It wasn't so far-fetched. I'd written. Even if very few had read me.

I think the receptionist phoned up to the jazz bar because she didn't quite catch my lack of credentials. I was welcome to go to the fourth floor and look around, but the bar wouldn't open for another hour.

The entrance was a dim, narrow passage. A black curtain not fully drawn revealed a sliver of bar ahead. Some plushy chair backs, the small not lit stage beyond, a drum kit on it. There was the distant sound of a vacuum coming on, then suddenly off. The darkened, empty bar evoked Stanley Kubrick anxieties and I was about to call out—almost Shelly Duvall shrilly—for someone, when a slim Japanese man in a trim dark suit emerged spookily yet not threateningly out of nowhere; less *The Shining*, more *Scooby Doo*.

He didn't miss the quality of my outfit, my hiking shoes. I was a journalist, I explained. This was somehow less impressive than I intended. I scrambled to produce some questions.

All I learned was that the band went on at nine. I'd be returning to see them, I explained. He pursed his lips, nodded. Did they have discounts for journalists, special drink prices, maybe? They did not.

Chutzpah, I've since discovered, isn't a particularly Japanese quality. One reason perhaps why the unhappy man let me look around after I asked. Also, it wouldn't cost him anything. I pulled my notebook from my knapsack, clicked on my 105-yen pen and wandered around the windowless room jotting notes, and doing it quick. My time was short, that was clear.

Walking toward the bar reminded me of going up the aisle at St. Peter's Basilica in Rome—a not dissimilar awe-inspiring experience. Of course, instead of Jesus on a cross you got single malt scotches lined in rows. There were also four giant champagne flute-shaped glass containers hanging above the bar, flames burning in each. I nearly missed the bartender quietly working away amongst the grandeur. He was happy to talk. The Mojito was their most popular drink, the 1947 Macallan the most expensive at $420 a glass.

As I was leaving, a burly Caucasian man entered wearing the kind of dirtied three-quarter length white coat that suggested he had either just come out of surgery or he worked in a kitchen. I approached because of his warm smile. Franz was the executive head chef in charge of all five of the hotel's restaurants. He was, with the soft brown eyes and confident belly of a good father, glad to talk to me. But could I come back later? He'd meet me at The Oak Door, the hotel's steak restaurant, at 6:30.

The movie itself was a bore. What's more, you hit a point in life when you realize you aren't George Clooney; you're no movie star. After that it's harder for movies to work their magic. How often can films' fairy dust still swirl once we've returned to the harsh light of the real adult world? Once you're old enough to know cool is but a synonym for good-looking and uncaring.

The upside is you stop pretending. You stop smoking.

That said, hope springs eternal, even for unqualified teachers, especially when they have somewhere to be and it being one of the swankiest steak joints in town. The fairy dust, in other words, would still a-swirl.

The restaurant was low-lit and high-ceilinged. Across from the entrance, an open kitchen where an international staff grilled obscenely priced cuts of cow. Two hostesses, like *Catch Me If You Can* flight attendants of a different era, beautiful, unwaveringly polite, led me to the bar after I stated my business.

I hid my knapsack at the foot of my stool. It didn't matter. The bartender summarily ignored me after I'd said I was "Okay for now." (The rich get richer and the rest of us perpetually in a state of "okay for now.")

Franz appeared decked out in his tall, white chef's hat to match the coat. He wasn't unfriendly but didn't sit. That worried me. It worried me worse when he enquired about my credentials. Had I even contacted the hotel's PR people? He couldn't say much, he explained, unless I went through the proper channels. I understood. I was a fraud. He was a busy man. "If you could kindly escort yourself out," was next.

It was a long walk back to the subway and I had two more connections before returning to my cruddy budget hotel. Except Franz wasn't kicking me out nor even chilling to my inexperience. Instead he asked what I was drinking.

Mojito was my first thought. Then scotch, scotch, scotch like a ticker tape across my brain. But Franz was such a nice guy; I felt a louse trying to weasel my way into fancy drinks that cost upwards of $15.

"A beer?" I said.

I wasn't a total con man. I really was passionate about great food and lush hotels. The writer's dream was real too, and maybe he saw that in me, maybe he was genuinely trying to help a kid begin to chart his course. I asked how he got his start, scribbling like mad to keep up. There was no order to my questions, nor did they add up to anything, but Franz didn't seem to mind. He got talking about the quality of ingredients in Japan, the best he'd worked with. The fish, of course, but also the meat, the tomatoes. He saw the disbelief on my face. The supermarket tomatoes in Osaka were disturbingly perfect-looking and totally flavourless. Had I ever had a tomato from Kumamoto? Franz turned for a waiter. One surfaced out of nowhere as they are trained to in five-star establishments. Soon a tomato, halved, was on a plate in front of me, shaved *daikon* radish piled unobtrusively to the side. The salt, of the pebble variety, was served in a silver dish. Beside my glass of Kirin lager, a plate with a slice of sourdough bread, a dish with a few pats of butter.

The tomato was a deep, profound red. I sprinkled some salt and knife and forked a bite, careful to then select a phrase to accurately express to the Tokyo Grand Hyatt's Head Chef the effect this had on me.

"*Oh my God*, Franz." It seemed important to add his name.

He wasn't fazed but was sorry, he had to go, other restaurants to oversee. He said to contact PR next time so I could have free reign of the hotel. I said I would and thanked him with the most pumping handshake I could muster.

I stayed a good half hour longer, nursing my food and drink in what is supposedly the best steakhouse in Tokyo. I wouldn't know, not on a conversation teacher's salary. It didn't matter. Because for that moment, with tomato, beer, and a slice of sourdough, it was all the glitter and glamour you could wish for. This was my 1947 glass of Macallan. This was my escape, my recharge, what I needed to continue.

I feel compelled to tell you I returned to the jazz bar later that night. I had to pay for my drink.

# DEFENSE/OFFENSE
## — *Hanorah Hanley* —
### POETRY

My nails grow long in memory of the men
Who've held tight to my wrists.

My tongue shrinks—
She shrinks and shrinks and shrinks, to not get bit.
My skirts are wide and wash down from my waist
A parachute, a padlock, a magic cape.

My eyes recall horror stories,
From lashes to mind
To make sure you colour within the lines
Infectious anger, a viral slime which will use your walls to climb

Like they've used mine.

# TWEET
## — *Jessica Kluthe* —
### FICTION

THE ACHE in her knuckles, a bone-deep pain when she bent her fingers or grasped or gripped, reminded her of all those days in the field: pulling, picking, planting.

She reached for the last of jar of her famous canned peaches from the storage room shelf and wrapped her hands around it. Her cursive stretched across the sticker on the glass: "Summer 2017." She remembered the exact day she made them because it was also the day that her pet bird, Brinkley, had died. She found him lying on his side on the newspaper that lined the bottom of his cage. When she was staring into the cage, she was sure dead Brinkley said "tweet" – not as a sound, the way birds do, but as a matter-of-fact word. When her grandson called later that night, she told him about the bird speaking because it had left her so bewildered.

Her grandson said, "You're serious?"

She said, "He spoke, but he was dead."

He said, "Tell me this again so I can tweet it."

And she did. She told the story again, but slowly. She added in more details about the day. And then she said, "Okay, let me hear your bird noises, let me hear you tweet," but he just laughed before saying goodbye.

And today, as she thought of Brinkley speaking again, she stared at the word 'summer' written in her familiar, bubbly cursive. The shape of the words, her letters, were as much a part of her as the sunspots on her hands or the roundness of her shoulders. But now, well, now she couldn't even press down a pencil hard enough to form letters on a page. And that was another kind of ache.

She wondered about all those digital words in typefaces that looked like everyone else's—she thought of the Times New Roman letters that arrived from her grandson on her birthday to the email she rarely checked. But she wondered, what would happen to her if she pressed her fingers down on the keyboard and plucked out words, line by line.

# PORCH SESSIONS
## — Jacalyn den Haan —
### FICTION

ONCE UPON a falling evening, in the days when I could still rise effortlessly from my swing and get through my mother's chore list, I thought sadness had trapped me on this porch. My heart pulsed purple and blue because of the hired hand, and my sister tried to console me but her baby was five months along and she couldn't understand. Above me, the sky burned a brilliant red. My watery eyes were furious with the beauty of the evening.

These days, my skin slips lower beneath my eyes as I sit through brimming sunsets, gazing from the porch of my farmhouse at the still-brilliant sun, my blanket gathered around me, my wheelchair right beside me. Memories of my youth waft back to me. My stooping husband emerges from the glow, strolling towards me, cap to the side, grey hair tufting out, half-grin. His lips curl down to kiss me. It's one of those kisses that contains passion and years of raw commitment. He tucks the blankets around me a little tighter, and still, even after the interim of time, there is safety in his presence. The scent of dirt from the fields drifts around me. A cooler breeze brings me closer into my blanket. Today the mid-May sun hovered over our fields, putting a song on my husband's lips as he worked the plough. The metal tillers cut into the soil and churned up the winter's weeds, spitting dust and dirt into the arid atmosphere. At 12:30 when the sun was at its highest, he came in singing, cracking jokes and making me laugh—even though my side still hurt from surgery. Now, the chill of evening brings silence to his machines. The dust settles once again over the land.

\* \* \*

My grandchildren say our world is caving in because we've corrupted the stardust, because the remnants of nebulas and supernovas that millions of years ago formed into granite and ribbons of coal have been pulverized into dust in the atmosphere. Because the air over Fort Saskatchewan that once was so pure is now nearly irreversibly polluted from oil and sand and industry. We will never get it back, they say, for we have a thousand good years left before we destroy ourselves from smog and dust.

From dust we came and to dust I know we must return, but these words make me wonder: what happens to that dust? Sadie, my second oldest grandchild, told me that we are churning the ground into particulate matter with our movement. It suspends itself in our lungs and penetrates our bloodstream. So it's turning dirt over to plant canola, the ambulance screaming down the highway to our house, that's causing my cough to deepen during the dry spells. Should I stop moving and pass away sooner to protect my grandchildren?

The particles enter the sky, Sadie says, and far, far up there in the atmosphere, they sit among the clouds. Evening sunlight reverberates against them, dazzles the eye as each ray scatters a million shades of salmon, orange, magenta, red. It's true what she says: tonight the clouds burst upon the dimming sky, and I can't remember a time when the sunset has been this brilliant. I call my husband onto the porch. He puts down the paper, comes outside, puts his hand lightly on my shoulder, and drinks it in with me. Even at 75, we are still brought to silence by the glow of the sunset.

People say that if something is beautiful, it is trustworthy and good. I rock back and forth in my swing underneath the burgundy evening and wonder how this can possibly be trustworthy. Nothing is more beautiful than this, but how can I put my trust in the death this beauty brings? How can my collapsing earth be something that I put my hope in—there is no hope in premature death, just a slammed door, a sentence cut halfway through, a phantom limb. When I pass on, my husband will spend weeks beside the tombstone feeling numb and years thinking he hears me just outside in my chair, reading or watching the planets spin. But if humanity passes, how will the birds respond? And the trees—will they mourn our loss? My memories of youth are coated with ethereal splendour, but this evening's sunset holds its own unreal beauty. The skyline burns a burnished orange over the rolling hills, and it feels like this sunset will absorb the world into itself: a supernova turned black hole, brilliant light swallowing up all that surrounds it into the deepest of nights.

I have learned to embrace thoughts of my own death. But I am too old to know whether my dear earth is dying. I don't study science. I myself am dying, with maybe ten years left but maybe a few days too, and who's to say either way. I have accepted my own fleeting memory, but can nothing be permanent? Even when I have been in the deepest pain, I have still put my hope in the life that will go on after my life—that my great-grandchildren will be free to dance through the corn fields during eternal summer afternoons, and not be threatened by microscopic particles lodging themselves in their fragile lungs.

The atmosphere burns in red and pink. I wonder what colours its redemption might take. The peace of my life has not come naturally; instead I've searched for it, and discovered joy was in letting go of my daydreams and my plans to carve my existence into the soil, and in realizing how beautiful was the absence of that which I'd wished for and did not find. I'm not wise enough to know how our actions can dampen the burning sunset, but perhaps we can learn to love letting go of what we expected out of life, of the roads we wanted to journey and the shortcuts we wanted to take that till our soil quickly but too heavily. There is beauty, too, in a slackened pace, the smell of fresh-turned soil, the rush of the wind in the poplars.

\* \* \*

Inside I can hear my husband snoring again. He will have let the newspaper fall to the ground beside his armchair. There will be a cold cup of decaf sitting on the little table next to him. In a few minutes I will need him to help me back into my wheelchair. In two days it will be time to seed, and maybe in a week's time I will have moved from a wheelchair to a cane. Maybe this change is here to stay. But when my youngest grandchildren come over tomorrow, I will tell them stories. I'll describe the sunset I saw tonight, get them to paint pictures of it for me. I will teach them about dust that hangs in the air like tiny balloons, that makes the sunset sing brilliantly but dangerously strong. I will teach them to move gently through this world. I will teach them the joy of letting go their need to conquer, to churn so quickly through life that they damage the world and themselves. I will teach them to love the peace of the present.

# THE WINTER AND I
## — *Erin Alladin* —
### POETRY

The winter and I have grown apart.
When I was small, I let it kiss my skin.
I rolled in its soft snow. It melted into me.
Now we only meet in passing at the bus stop,
Me bundled up against its touch, eyes down,
Missing that warm-blooded childhood innocence.
They say the climate's changing, but I think
This time the one who changed was me.

# MEET THE AUTHORS

**Trevor Abes** (pg. 35) is an artist from Toronto with a fondness for writing essays and poetry. He was part of the winning ensemble at the 2015 SLAMtario Spoken Word Festival, and competed in both the National Poetry Slam and the Canadian Festival of Spoken Word as part of the Toronto Poetry Slam team. His work has appeared in *Torontoist, (parenthetical), untethered magazine, Spacing* Magazine*, Descant* Magazine*, The Rusty Toque, The Theatre Reader, Mooney on Theatre, The Toronto Review of Books, Hart House Review,* and *Sequential: Canadian Comics News & Culture,* among others. Reach him on Instagram @TrevorAbes.

**Erin Alladin** (pg. 1, 95, 113, and 156) grew up in North Bay and Corbeil, Ontario, where her family did such charming old-fashioned things as tap maple trees, make patchwork quilts, and know wildflowers by name. Lured by literary grandeur, she wandered off the Canadian Shield and became the Associate Editor of Pajama Press in Toronto, but the woods is always calling to her. To placate her need for growing things, Erin founded Toronto's Garden@Kimbourne Community Permaculture Project. She also writes obsessively about roots—physical, metaphorical, and usually both at once.

**John Alpaugh** (pg 123) is a student at Dalhousie University, living in Halifax, Nova Scotia, in his final year of a degree in philosophy and physics. He is originally from Barrie, Ontario. John spent the summer of 2018 living in Ingonish, Nova Scotia, working on the grounds crew for the Cape Breton Highlands Links at the Keltic Lodge and exploring the Cape Breton Highlands National Park. This is his first time being published.

**Anna Baines** (pg 96) was born and raised in Calgary, AB where she currently resides with her fiancé, their dog, and their cat. She has been writing poetry for most of her life, using writing as both an emotional outlet and a way to seek out hidden meaning in mundane surroundings. Anna is passionate about mental health, having completed a Bachelor's of Arts in psychology at the University of Calgary. Mental illness and wellness are prevalent themes in much of her poetry. She also enjoys hiking in the Rocky Mountains and finds inspiration in the quiet reprieve of nature.

**Brianne Christensen** (pg 42) is a nineteen-year-old poet from Langley, BC. Apart from writing, Brianne loves her family, her dog, and cookie dough ice-cream. She currently lives in Kelowna, enrolled in her second year at the University of British Columbia, studying English. Published in her university anthology in the Spring of 2018, Brianne is just beginning her journey as a young author.

**Craig Clark** (pg. 19) is a writer and editor from Burlington, Ontario. His work has been featured in various publications including the *Toronto Star, TERN Magazine,* and *Medium*. He is passionate about education with a focus on the impact of media on youth and culture. He spent a lot of his early 20s travelling to diverse countries such as Australia, Japan, and Egypt. Currently, he is working on his first novel and enjoys spending time with his new baby Madeleine and wife Valeria. Twitter: @craigclark.

**Zeba Crook** (pg. 22) was born in Montreal and given an Iranian woman's name by his hippie mother. His boyhood included three years squatting in an abandoned log-mansion from the gold-rush days in the Shuswap Lake region of British Columbia. A first career on the Canadian National Track and Field Team took him around the world, and to university, which led to a second career in academia. He is now a Full Professor of Religious Studies at Carleton University in Ottawa.

**Yelibert Cruz** (pg. 60) is a Venezuelan poet and storyteller who grew up in Guelph, Ontario and is currently attending Wilfrid Laurier University. She has been published in Laurier's Blueprint Magazine. Recently she has been focusing on spoken word poetry and took part in the KWPS Residency, where she successfully competed for a spot on the KWPS slam team. Her artistic works stem from an anti-oppressive lens where she explores the many layers of feminism and body positivity from her unique Latin-Canadian perspective. Yeli can be found on Twitter @YelibertCruz or on Instagram @YeliWrites.

**Spencer Dawson** (pg. 40) writes out of Toronto Ontario where he lives and works as an electrician for Local 353. His first published piece, "Some Just Whine and Complain" can be read in the first volume of *Coffin Bell*. Other than a love for music and the environment there isn't much else to say about him. You can find retweets about all these things and more by following @SirSpennyD on twitter.

**Tracy Evans** (pg 133) is obsessed with story and the concept of "awe" and spends her time seeking more of both in the world. She was born and raised on the prairies and loves watching the horizon stretch to infinity. She teaches, writes, and explores the world from her home base in Calgary, Alberta, where she lives with her husband, two young children, and a deaf chihuahua. She loves playing outside and finds inspiration in unplugging and wandering whenever possible. She adores a good cup of coffee at sunrise and the opportunity to play with rearranging words. @evans306.

**Sheri Falconer** (pg. 75) enjoys writing for the sake of writing, exploring ideas and imagining what would be, playing with words to paint a picture, or maybe just picking up a brush to paint one. She relishes a hearty discussion, sharing stories, and playing with perspectives. She loves getting lost in a good book and dreams of seeing her own novels in print. When she's not writing, she's sewing, sketching, training for a triathlon, or perhaps just spending a quiet moment with her husband and two children at home in Hanover, Ontario. More of her writing can be found on her blog at dancingthroughthewaves.blogspot.ca/.

**Kristin Fast** (pg. 87) is a writer from Central Alberta. Living between the prairies and the mountains, she has plenty of opportunity to explore both the majestic and mundane. Her writing draws on myth and fairy tales, early modern and modernist styles, and a healthy dose of sensory exploration. She loves art that doesn't compromise but comports itself with flair. A web developer by day, she scribbles to the cheerful bounce of big band jazz in the evening. She holds an MA in English & Film Studies from the University of Alberta.

**Emily Fata** (pg. 31) is an author and blogger based in Toronto. She runs the travel and lifestyle blog Emulating Emily and has recently launched a travel website, Wanderous Affair. Her passion lies in writing: creating and formulating moving pieces from her experiences and the experiences of others. Emily has been published three times by the Poetry Institute of Canada, had her novel, *Amazing Grace,* published in November 2015, and has written multiple articles for Elite Daily and Thought Catalog. For more information on Emily, you can visit her website at emilymichellefata.com.

**Michael Foy** (pg. 44) was born and raised in Surrey, BC. He completed degrees in psychology and teaching at Simon Fraser University. He currently lives in Montréal with his wife and two daughters and teaches psychology at John Abbott College. He enjoys reading and writing short stories. His stories have appeared in *The Nashwaak Review, Grain,* and *The Impressment Gang.* He also has a cat named Prince, who reads all of his work.

**Rachel Freeman** (pg. 101) lives in Kitchener with her husband, two kids, and a pair of cats. She is an aspiring author who enjoys all manner of artistic expression. Creativity is a part of her everyday life and if music is playing, Rachel is singing along.

**Sarah Gardiner** (pg. 71) lives with her husband and two small children in Calgary, Alberta. Being a busy stay-at-home mom, she tries to use nap time as her creative opportunity to write, read, crochet, and cook. Writing has become a newfound love that allows her to escape and explore through new plots and characters. Her curiosity with people, possibilities, and forever asking 'what if?' seems to grow as her creative side continues to be challenged.

**Roq Gareau** (pg. 2) is co-author of *Soulful Fellowship: Men, Meaning and Purpose* and Director of CentreSpoke Consulting. *Soulful Fellowship* is Roq's first book, in which he explores essential reframings needed for men (and those that accompany them) to find belonging and wholeness in times like these. For the last ten years, Roq has also co-convened retreats at which men have been unpacking untellable stories and shameful life experiences to transform wound to gift and insight. Roq's work integrates aspects of his learning over the last 20 years—men's work, leadership, group facilitation, initiation and ritual. He lives in Comox, British Columbia.

**Rosalind Goldsmith** (pg. 92) lives in Toronto and has written for radio and theatre. She began writing short fiction several years ago. Since then her stories have appeared in the *Quilliad, Flash Fiction, Thrice Fiction, Litro UK, Popshot UK, Understorey* and *Filling Station, antilang., Burningwood Journal*, and others.

**Jacalyn den Haan** (pg. 152) is an emerging writer and education student from varying locations in Canada's west. She is passionate about giving young people opportunities to play with and construct a deeper understanding of language. While her primary mode is poetry, she also experiments with fiction and with editing. Her self-published chapbooks include *A Fragile Youth* and *Deep Creek*, a compilation of poetry and photography, and she is working on a third compilation of poetry, a memoir told through verse.

**Meaghan Hackinen** (pg. 91) is a writer, cyclist, and retired roller girl originally from the West Coast of British Columbia. A graduate of the University of Saskatchewan's MFA in Writing program, Meaghan's fiction and nonfiction prose explores relationships, experiences on the road, and encounters with wild places. Meaghan's work has appeared in *Cargo Lit Mag, Compose: A Journal of Simply Good Writing, The Feathertale Review* (forthcoming), *The Fieldstone Review, Momentum Mag, One Throne, untethered,* and *Poetry All Over the Floor*. Her travel memoir *South Away* will be published by NeWest Press in 2019. You can follow her adventures on Instagram @meaghanhackinen.

**Mark Halpern** (pg. 63) has lived since 1993 in Tokyo, where he runs his own law firm. He was born in America, mostly grew up in Canada, and has spent long periods in the UK and France. In 2016, Mark began writing short stories about foreigners living in Japan. In life, Mark has done enough foolish things to be capable of granting his stories' characters the same level of respect he grants himself. And, like some of them, in Japan he has found a way to be both an outsider and an insider.

**Hanorah Hanley** (pg. 74 and 149) is a 24-year-old multi-ethnic artist and advocate for consent based in Montreal. Although primarily a musician, she is also a visual artist and young writer. In 2016, she successfully campaigned for mandatory consent education at her *alma mater* John Abbott College. Her album, "Post-Romantic Stress Disorder" (2017), and frank discussion of sexual assault and mental health during her appearance on Canada's "The Voice," on which she was a quarter-finalist, have put her on Journal de Montréal's "2018's

Most Inspiring Quebec Women" list. She is completing her undergrad in Studio Arts at Concordia University and signed with Dare to Care Records in 2018.

**Jennie Hunter** (pg. 114) is an emerging writer and a member of the Saskatchewan Writer's Guild. Her literary work has previously appeared on Broken Pencil Magazine On-line. When she isn't writing, she works in the field of Environmental Engineering. She is currently working on a selection of stories that involve women in non-tradition roles. Jennie Hunter was thankful to receive a grant from the Saskatchewan Arts Board in 2018.

**Desiree Kendrick** (pg. 88) A graduate of The University of Alberta Desiree fused her Bachelor of Arts degree with a Project Management certificate. By day she's an Event Planner. She was a runner-up in the 2018 "Heritage Writing Competition," with her article, "The Spirit of Apulia" (https://seniortravelexpert.com/) and her prose, "I Hate My Mother," was included in Nod magazine's 24th edition. She is currently working on a novel.

**Jessica Kluthe** (pg. 150) named one of Edmonton's Top 40 Under 40, is an instructor at MacEwan University and the co-creator of the Third-Verb writing workshops. Kluthe completed a MFA in Writing at the University of Victoria in 2011. Two years later, her first book, *Rosina, The Midwife* landed on the *Edmonton Journal's* list of bestsellers for over ten weeks; in addition, an early chapter of her book was a finalist for the Writers Guild of Alberta's James H. Grab Award for Short Nonfiction in 2011 and the Wilfrid Eggleston Award for Nonfiction in 2014. Since the publication of *Rosina, The Midwife*, Jessica has been published in four print anthologies as well as *Avenue Magazine* and *Little Fiction*.

**Kim Losier** (pg. 138) was born in Saint John, New Brunswick and attended Mount Saint Vincent University in Halifax. Kim retired in June 2016 after a thirty-eight year career in the Tele-communication industry. Aside from writing, Kim is very active in her church community, serving on the Creative Arts and Media team, and has an intense love of music. Kim has been writing poetry, creative nonfiction and personal memoirs for many years. Her writings are inspired by her personal life experiences and are often laced with wonderful humour. Kim enjoys her summers with family and her dog Riley at her summer residence in Whitehead, NB, on the Kingston Peninsula overlooking the beautiful Kennebecasis River.

**Kelly-Anne Maddox** (pg. 80) is a creative nonfiction writer whose current work focuses mainly on memoir. She previously wrote a monthly political satire column for *Off-Centre Magazine* and contributed several guest posts to the *Local Tourist Ottawa* blog. In her spare time she's into hiking, powerlifting, and reading Scandinavian and Icelandic murder mysteries. She lives in Ottawa with her husband and two children.

**Heather McLeod** (pg. 127) currently lives in Toronto, Ontario, Canada with her partner and their three sons. She currently makes ends meet as an educator, writing in any and all of the spare time she can find. She is working on a novel and a collection of short stories.

**Jonathan Mendelsohn** (pg. 144) When he isn't working as an adjunct professor of applied linguistics at York University, Jonathan Mendelsohn writes fiction and creative non-fiction. He has previously published short fiction in *Prism International* and creative non-fiction in a variety of publications including *The Toronto Review of Books, Today's Parent, Cha: An Asian Literary Review, The Globe and Mail*, and *The Toronto Star*. He has also served on a jury for the Ve'ahavta Creative Writing contest and is currently on the selection committee for the Toronto South African Film Festival. His novel, ANA BEGINS, is a coming-of-age love story set in Japan.

**Tamzin Mitchell** (pg. 99) is an American-British-Canadian proofreader and editor with a chronic case of wanderlust. She holds an MFA from the University of New Hampshire and has been nominated for Best of the Net and the Pushcart Prize. Her fiction and nonfiction have appeared in *Waxwing, Cosmonauts Avenue, cahoodaloodaling, Crannóg*, and elsewhere.

**Harvey Mitro** (pg. 53) is a husband and father who lives in Toronto. As a personal trainer, he has guided exercise for people ranging from age 4 to 101. He has been a runner for over thirty years, has broken four-minutes for the mile, and has represented Canada internationally. He offers this piece from his first foray into writing, part of a collection of 28 works to be entitled, "Taking Life in Stride."

**Candace Janelle Ormond** (pg. 130) is a social profit worker in Wood Buffalo and mother of two. Originally from Cape Breton, she completed her BA from St. Francis Xavier University in 2012 and made the permanent move to the Great North immediately after. In her spare time, Candace enjoys being outdoors or following her passion for creative pursuits such as writing and painting. She is fascinated with the human condition, often writing about experience and relationships. She recently completed her first manuscript.

**David Perlmutter** (pg. 135) is a freelance writer based in Winnipeg, Manitoba. He is the author of *America Toons In: A History of Television Animation* (McFarland and Co.), *The Singular Adventures Of Jefferson Ball* (Chupa Cabra House), *The Pups* (Booklocker.com), *Certain Private Conversations and Other Stories* (Aurora Publishing), *Honey and Salt* (Scarlet Leaf Publishing), *The Encyclopedia of American Animated Cartoon Series* (Rowman and Littlefield) and *Orthicon; or, the History of a Bad Idea* (Linkville Press, forthcoming) He can be reached on Facebook at David Perlmutter-Writer, Twitter at @DKPLJW1, and Tumblr at The Musings of David Perlmutter (yesdavidperlmutterfan).

**Hina Rani** (pg. 141) has no idea how to read tarot cards. She apologizes profusely to the members of the clairvoyant community for any inaccurate depictions of fortune-telling in this story. Aside from not predicting the future, her interests include loud music, ghost stories, and engaging in general tomfoolery.

**Jordan Ryder** (pg. 57) is from Toronto, Ontario. She's just spent a year in Ireland where she drank loads of Guinness and studied for her Master's degree in Literature and Publishing. Jordan received her MA with First Class Honours from the National University of Ireland, Galway, and she also holds a BA in Creative Writing from Dalhousie University, in Halifax. Currently, Jordan is working for the Brink Literacy Project and trying to figure out how to be a professional. She writes whenever she can and is adamant that a manuscript is on its way.

**Nicole Schroeder** (pg. 104) Fuelled by coffee, chocolate milk, and the grace of God, Nicole wakes each morning ready to chase twin four-year-old boys, laugh wildly with her husband, and search desperately for her car keys. Catch up with Nicole over at https://introvertedperspective.wordpress.com

**Susan Siddeley** (pg. 83) graduated with a B.A. Hons degree in Politics and a Diploma in Education from the University of Wales. After emigrating with her geologist husband to Canada, she spent many years in Jamaica, Bolivia, and Chile. Now back in Toronto, Susan enjoys the vibrant writing scene and opportunity to reflect and write of her experiences in a changing world. She has written four poetry chapbooks, a memoir, *Home First*, and is working on a sequel, *Without a Map*.

**Sheri Singleton** (pg. 21) is a graduate of Memorial University and teaches High School English. She lives with her two cats on the beautiful island of Twillingate, NL, a picturesque community of roughly 2500 people off the province's northeast coast. Her poem, "The Drive", appears in the English 3202 text *Vistas* used by grade 12 students province wide. She is currently working on her first novel.

**Stephanie Tamagi** (pg. 27) is an Alberta-born author, though her roots began elsewhere. A freelance writer and novelist, her work has previously appeared in *Other Voices* magazine. She loves to disappear into books, play in the dirt and kitchen, and watch all things grow. Stephanie's varied work history, from painter to project manager, provides rich inspiration for her writing. She holds a degree in Political Science and Creative Writing from the University of Alberta. Stephanie can often be found living in her head, which currently resides somewhere around Edmonton.

**Alyssa Thiessen** (pg. 111) is a writer and a teacher hailing from the vibrant centre of Canada. She teaches high school in southern Manitoba, and her work can be found in a number of Canadian magazines and anthologies. She has also authored three Young Adult novels. Although she loves the beauty of the written word and the thrill of engaging learners, her greatest joy is found in her family. She currently resides in Winnipeg, Manitoba with her husband, their three children, and their Miniature Schnauzer.

**Jennifer Turney** (pg. 84) lives in Huntsville, Ontario, where she can usually be found exploring nature and the outdoors with her three very active kids (and her husband). She writes a little bit of everything: flash fiction, short stories, poetry, novels, and screenplays, and has participated in the Muskoka Novel Marathon the last four years in a row. She bakes an amazing, award-winning zucchini bread and is actually a ninja-in-training.

**Cynthia Scott Wandler** (pg. 37) has been published in *The Hopper*, the *#yegwords Coffee Sleeve Project, borrowed solace, Understorey Magazine,* and *Far Off Places!* Her essay, "Things You Can't Do With a Broken Left Arm", won the 2018 Jon Whyte Memorial Essay Alberta Literary Award. She lives in Morinville, Alberta, where she runs an environmental program with the town and advocates for children's brain health. She would love for you to say hi at www.cynthiascottwandler.ca

**Corals Zheng** (pg. 109) is an English literature and Political Science double major at the University of Toronto. While her preoccupation is academic research, she loves to write Anne-Carson-style prose essays about uninteresting observations and the day-to-day microaggressions that comes with living in urban spaces. Zheng is an avid traveller of formerly (and currently) communist countries, an urban beekeeper, illustrator for *The Varsity*, paddle-boater, and hiker.

Enjoy *Blank Spaces* to its full potential! Visit **blankspaces.ca** and subscribe to receive a beautiful, full colour celebration of Canadian talent, delivered to your mailbox every quarter.

Made in the USA
Columbia, SC
16 September 2019